Valuegraphics uses big data to unlock the shared values of large groups of people. It's an astonishingly effective audience profiling tool because what we value determines what we do.

Valuegraphics increases budget effectiveness as much as eight times, creates audience profiles with data instead of guesswork, mitigates the risk of innovation, decreases internal politics around key decisions, and prepares organizations in any sector with crucial insights as they face disruption.

We Are All the Same Age Now is a comprehensive guide explaining how Valuegraphics was created and what it can do. It includes a DIY system that starts you on the road to using Valuegraphics instead of demographics to guide brainstorming and decision-making throughout your organization.

Valuegraphics is the big data tool we've all been waiting for. We can now start to build a world based on shared values that bring us together instead of the vague and outdated demographic stereotypes that drive us apart.

ADVANCE PRAISE

"Valuegraphics are destined to reduce wasted effort, time, and money."

"Valuegraphics are the missing link we need to move beyond demographic stereotyping."

"On Wall Street or Main Street, it's so much better to face a client with strategies based on real audience data, instead of demographic stereotypes that just don't hold water anymore."

"Design is a language based on fully understanding the end user. Finally we have some real information to work with."

"It's hard to tell what's better: the statistical proof that generational stereotypes are inaccurate, or that David Allison has come up with a new way to profile audiences with eight times more accuracy. You'll have to read the book and decide for yourself."

—ERIC TERMUENDE, COFOUNDER OF NOW INNOVATIONS AND BEST-SELLING AUTHOR OF *RETHINK WORK*

"We've been reliant on a lot of opinion and intuition to make good things. Now we can get more precise about what people care about, and what they don't."

—WALKER MCKINLEY, ARCHITECT AT AAA AIBC MAA OAA MRAIC MARCH MDES AND PARTNER AT MCKINLEY BURKART ARCHITECTS

"This book, this discovery, will mean rewriting the Marketing 101 textbooks."

—KALYM LIPSEY, MARKET RESEARCHER AND PHD CANDIDATE (SOCIOLOGY, MASSEY UNIVERSITY, NEW ZEALAND)

"David just gets it. It's a rare skill."

—ANTHONY VON MANDL, PROPRIETOR OF VMF FAMILY ESTATES AND CHAIRMAN AND CEO OF MARK ANTHONY BRANDS

"David's work and ideas help increase sales velocity and price. He adds to the ROI of your project."

—ROB MACDONALD, CEO OF MACDONALD DEVELOPMENT CORPORATION

WE ARE ALL THE SAME AGE NOW

We Are All the Same Age Now

VALUEGRAPHICS
The End of Demographic Stereotypes

David Allison

LIONCREST
PUBLISHING

WE ARE ALL THE SAME AGE NOW
Valuegraphics, The End of Demographic Stereotypes

ISBN   978-1-5445-0087-4 *Paperback*
       978-1-5445-0086-7 *Ebook*

CONTENTS

THANKS

So many people, listed here in alphabetical order, helped me in so many ways: Niels and Nancy Bendtsen, Ben Chick, Kyle Dunn, Cathy Grant, Callum Gunn, Harry Hill, Ryan Laurin, Kalym Lipsey, Diana McMeekin, Donna Molby, Jean Oplinger, Greg Smith, Eric Termuende, Cam Wharram, everyone at the National Speakers Bureau and the Global Speakers Agency, all my clients, and my family.

Special thanks to Douglas Coupland for his editorial help on this book and for writing *Generation X* all those years ago. That book changed my life back then and continues to do so now.

The most special thanks of all goes to Chris Nicholson, who provides unfathomable love and support. XO114

NOBODY ACTS THEIR AGE ANYMORE

HELLO

I've found something quite simple that could change the world.

To be perfectly clear, the idea is quite simple, the research behind it was incredibly complex, and its ramifications are potentially profound.

Here's what I mean.

We've now reached a point in history when people no longer act their age. You can marry someone for the first time and simultaneously start a third career while in your seventies. You might also be the CEO of a Fortune 500 company before your thirtieth birthday, decide to remain single, and adopt three kids from three different Eastern European countries.

For various reasons I'll touch on later, I had noticed this new agelessness changing the world around me and commissioned a study to prove a hunch. I hoped to prove that using age to predict how people would behave didn't really make sense anymore.

I also wanted to see if we could find a more contemporary and accurate way to profile target audiences. Age as a profiling tool is an idea well past its best-before date, as far as I'm concerned. It's time to take age out of the back of the metaphorical refrigerator and toss it in the rubbish heap of history.

Good news. We found the proof we were looking for, that age is a lousy way to predict what anyone is going to do. So that worked out. And we also built a system to profile target audiences based on what people value. So that means we are two for two.

Now, as much as I'd like to claim it as mine, the idea that *what we value determines what we do* is nothing new. Psychologists, sociologists, and consumer behavior experts have studied this from every conceivable angle for a long time. We know it's true.

The problem has always been that there wasn't an accurate way to profile the values of an entire target audience. To profile an entire audience on a national or even a merely regional scale, you'd need a gigantic amount of data, or any profile you came up with would only be marginally better than a guess.

No one built that enormous pile of data before now because it would have been insanely complex and expensive. Most of the cost would have been from finding enough people to fill out surveys so your database was statistically large enough to be accurate.

Until now, finding qualified survey respondents has always been about teams of people with clipboards inefficiently accosting random passersby in shopping malls. Or call centers full of bored telemarketers phoning people at home precisely when dinner is served until they find enough folks who are willing to let their roast beef or buttered chicken go cold while they answer questions that "won't take more than a few moments of your time." More recently, it's become possible to carpet-bomb emails to lists of people sourced from various places with only a micropercentage of those surveys ever filled out and sent back in. All that failure to find qualified participants costs a lot of money and takes a lot of people a lot of time.

But today, enormous social media companies keep whole buildings full of the smartest and best-paid scientists on the planet who do nothing but develop algorithms to help advertisers precisely target their messages. This is a key point because it turns out those algorithms are equally as handy for finding survey respondents who fit precise qualifications for a study. Thanks to those algorithms, instead of an entire team, I was able to work with only one researcher to recruit 40,000 qualified survey respondents* and save uncounted millions of dollars and years of work. How much time and money we saved will never be known for certain, but regardless, let's have a

---

* And we keep adding more. As of this writing, we have reached 75,000 survey responses.

big round of applause for our new friend, algorithmic technology. Thanks to those algorithms, age is out, and values are in.

There is one last monster I want to slay before we carry on: the surveys themselves. Despite how much I talk about our surveys in the following pages, you won't find a copy of our full survey anywhere in this book. But since I don't want you to spend your time wondering about the omission while reading this book, I've provided a small example of a few survey questions, along with the following explanation.

Our surveys were web based, which means they didn't have to be linear. If someone answered yes to the first question, they'd see a second question that varied depending on several factors. Depending on how they answered that question, they might see any one of three or four follow-up questions, or possibly a question about something entirely different. And on and on it went, up to a total potential of 340 questions, depending on how you answered.

To complicate matters further, there were ten surveys organized by various themes around the forty values we were interested in knowing more about. If you tried to draw one of these surveys on a piece of paper, it would look like an elaborate spiderweb, but in 3-D. So there's really no way to show you even a single survey, let alone all ten, until books become capable of showing more than two dimensions.

However, because some people really want to know these things, I've included below the questions around just one topic, from just one of the ten surveys, about just one of the possible themes we explored around the forty values in our work.

This tiny sample of the full survey is here to illustrate the depth and breadth of the information we captured from the survey respondents and gives you some sense of the immense dataset we have collected. What follows are the questions we would ask of someone who had indicated some interest in fan loyalty in the thematic survey about sports and fitness.

As you skim through this very small example, note how some of the questions help us understand the respondent's attitude toward the obvious: sports team loyalty. But also watch for how we learn about loyalty in general, about possessions, about family, and through some of the open-ended questions, about a host of other values the respondent finds important.

FAN LOYALTY AND NUMBER OF TEAMS SUPPORTED: A SAMPLE SURVEY

Those who indicated they support sports teams were asked a combination of the following questions:

1. In the past twelve months, what percentage of your team's home games have you attended?
    a. 100 percent

b. Between 75 percent and 100 percent

c. Between 50 percent and 75 percent

d. Between 25 percent and 50 percent

e. Less than 25 percent

f. None

2. In the past twelve months, have you attended any away games?

a. No

b. Yes, five or more

c. Yes, three or four

d. Yes, one or two

3. Who do you attend games with? Please select all that apply.

a. Family

b. Friends

c. Work colleagues

d. Supporters group/club

e. Other (please specify):

4. For as long as you have watched *insert sport here*, have you always supported *insert club/team here*?

a. Yes.

b. No. I previously supported a different club/team.

5. What was the primary reason why you changed the team/club you support?

6. Do you have a second favorite team/club?
   a. Yes, always.
   b. Yes, only if my team/club gets eliminated from playoffs/finals.
   c. No.

7. Have you ever found yourself in a verbal argument in support of your favorite team/club?
   a. Yes, more than once.
   b. Yes, once.
   c. No.

8. What about a physical altercation?
   a. Yes, more than once.
   b. Yes, once.
   c. No.

9. Do your family members support the same team/club as you?
   a. Yes, all.
   b. Yes, some.
   c. No.
   d. Don't know.

10. Which of the following do you own? Please select all that apply. (Full list of common merchandise items depending on the sport.)

11. Approximately how much have you spent on *insert team name* merchandise in the past twelve months?

12. Please rate your level of agreement with each of the following statements: (0–10 rating)
    a. "I would still support my favorite team/club if they changed cities."
    b. "I would still support my favorite team/club if my favorite player left."

Now that we've got all that out of the way, let's get on with the show. We will start in the distant past.

A BRIEF HISTORY OF AGE

If we go way back into history, into the furthest reaches of time, we know that age played a vital role in how society policed itself.

Before the advent of the calendar, your maturity was measured by the number of babies you'd produced, the number of harvests you'd been part of, or the number of enemies you'd sliced open in battle. Societal pressures to act your age were strictly enforced, and penalties for not playing along were severe.

If a young woman didn't marry after a certain number of harvests or cycles of the moon, she was obviously a witch or a demon, which gave the Inquisition something to do. Meanwhile, unmarried men of a certain age were sent off to a monastery to live with other thoughtful, quiet boys of their kind.

It was a matter of life and death to keep things ticking along in a timely fashion. If we didn't cram everything possible into our incredibly short lifespan and produce enough babies, weapons, and backup food reserves, we were in danger of being attacked by our enemies from the next village down the road who could smell weakness on the back of a summer breeze. Age was the best way to make sure everyone knew what they were expected to do and when.

Fast-forward a few millennia to the recent past. Things had changed, but not entirely. Age was still bossy. Even one generation ago, when my parents were young, there was overwhelming pressure from society, family, and friends to be married by a certain age and have kids. Why? Because it's what everyone did, or they risked mass shunning.

I talked to one couple, who are now in their seventies, who decided not to have kids when they got married over forty years ago. It's an eye-opener how they were treated. They were called selfish right to their face. More than once, the name of a fertility doctor was slipped surreptitiously into her purse or his pocket by a well-meaning friend or family member.

Thanks to all that shaming, the vast majority of the North American population fell in line and followed the age-based rules of the day. They got married after graduating from high school, moved to a house in the suburbs, and in quick succession, had at least two babies. Producing more was admirable and referred to as a blessing. On the other hand, having only one child caused speculation at PTA meetings about whose reproductive organs had crapped out early, his or hers. There was no doubt about it, two was definitely the right number of progeny.

Mortality rates for men peaked early because of cutthroat office politics, the pressure of supporting the family on one income, and the daily commute between the city and a house in the suburbs they couldn't quite afford. Unhappy, stagnating, and stressed, like the characters in a John Cheever novel, these men lived gin-soaked lives of quiet desperation in the alienating social ecosystem of the suburbs.

Accompanied by the sound of a million sprinklers sput-sputtering over a million lawns, the women had their own age-based rituals to follow. First, they were new brides, and then they quite quickly morphed into expectant mothers. After kindergarten provided relief from the responsibilities of round-the-clock child-rearing, many became bored. They watched soap operas, which we invented to help housewives feel like they were part of a much more exciting family, in which time was passing in a narrative sense. They did the ironing. Once a week, they got together to knit, drink, play cards, and talk about their favorite soap operas. Those TV lives were much more interesting than the ones they were leading themselves.

Today, we are in the midst of a transition away from the rigid age-based rituals of the past. We're moving on to something not yet fully understood but definitely new. Today, we routinely talk about how fifty is the new thirty, and sixty is the new forty. Most people have friends of all ages, which would have seemed odd a half century ago. Societal rules about behaving a certain way at a certain time in your life are, today, fairly easily ignored.

Here's an example.

My friend Gordon Smith is a very deservedly famous painter who has artworks hanging in important public and private collections around the world. The Queen of England recently unveiled one of his paintings that was chosen for the Canadian Embassy in London. Gordon paints six hours a day, seven days a week. His art dealer mounts an exhibition of his work every year in October, and the paintings sell almost immediately, with six-digit price tags attached.

Gordon and I drink whiskey and sneak the occasional cigar (shhh!). We talk about everything from being boy scouts and having newspaper routes as kids to our favorite plays and films to the best stores for socks in London. We also talk a lot about the Second World War because Gordon was there. You see, he's ninety-eight this year. No one has told him he is too old to be a busy and successful artist. He'd probably throw something at them if they did.

And it's not only the elders among us who are winning the battle against these age-based stereotypes. Incredibly capable and intelligent young people are being encouraged to be the best version of themselves from early on too.

Here's another example.

Last summer, I met the most remarkable fellow in Berlin. His name is Mihir Garimella. Three years ago, he entered and won a global competition organized by Google to promote scientific innovation.

Mihir submitted a comprehensive study of the flight patterns of fruit flies. His hypothesis was that flying robots capable of the same aeronautical maneuvers as the fruit flies could be quite useful. He won the competition, and the next thing he knew, he was working with MIT and Stanford to build his flying robots. Today, Mihir's robots go into impossible places, like buildings that have collapsed after an earthquake or a bomb, to see if there's anyone left alive. Mihir was seventeen when I met him. He was fourteen when he entered the Google Science Fair and won. Nobody told him he was too young to make robots that save lives.

All this talk of age being less important than it once was is encouraging, except for one astounding fact.

In every boardroom in every organization around the world, age is still the basis for creating stereotypes, otherwise referred to as audience profiles or personas. We need these so we can understand who we are trying to sell things to. We still assume people of a certain age will behave a certain way, and we spend trillions of dollars of human and financial resources accordingly. We can't seem to stop ourselves from age-based profiling. Other demographics get their share of the blame too, but age is the stereotyping alpha.

Madison Avenue advertising agencies love age-based conformity. It's easier to sell things to people when they act a certain way at a certain age because it's predictable. Insurance companies are big fans too, still basing their risk calculations on ideas about who does what at a certain age. It would be so much easier for these and other billion-dollar industries if we would all continue acting our age.

But what I've discovered will turn their world upside down. If I'm found bludgeoned to death by a fax machine, splayed out in a pool of blood in the back room of an Office Depot in New Jersey a few months after this book is released, watch the global advertising and insurance conglomerates for shifty behavior. One of my mentors wonders why I haven't been dismembered already, given the blogging I've been doing while working on this book for the last two years. My work is going to mess some things up in a serious way, and not everyone will be happy about it.

The fact is, age-based stereotypes are still used to design, manufacture, and sell televisions, cars, noise-canceling headphones, and bottled water to stereotypical people who no longer exist. Trillions of dollars are riding on faulty logic.

We've all been doing this for so long now that most people have memorized a standard set of age categories. I bet you can recite these anytime the subject comes up:

| 18 to 24 | 25 to 36 | 37 to 45 | 46 to 54 | 55 to 69 | And finally, 70+ |

Where did those categories come from? Why do they stop at seventy? Who decided that forty-five-year-olds suddenly became something else once they turned forty-six?

We even give those categories cute names like we do with pets or favorite cars. We have boomers, zoomers, millennials, and of course Generations X, Y, and Z.

Have you heard about perennials and Xennials? They are googleable things now with their own proponents, support groups, and specialist consultants for hire. By the time this book is printed, I bet you a slice of birthday cake that a half dozen new age categories will have popped up. And all of them will be equally useless *because you are not your age*. None of us are.

The reason age-based profiles have lasted so long is because we didn't have an alternative. We had to profile audiences somehow, and choosing an age category seemed to make sense.

But this is exactly like wearing a pair of those chunky black-framed eyeglasses with nonprescription lenses. Those big fake spectacles might make you look smart, but they aren't really improving your vision.

AN UNINTENTIONAL OUTCOME

Like 3M Post-it Notes, Viagra, and microwave ovens, the research discovery that prompted me to write this book was a bit of a fluke. It will help you answer some questions you might have if you know a little bit about my background and about how I ended up in the middle of all this.

I grew up in the Prairies, where we feared winter and mosquitoes, and worked hard every day. I went to university and studied journalism because telling a good story about the truth was an honorable profession. Then I disappointed my journalism professors by going to work on the dark side, in advertising and marketing, and using my skills to help several large global brands tell the stories they wanted to tell. Before I knew it, I was thirty-one years old and had a career that alternated between dull and stressful.

I thought the solution might be to start my own marketing company, so that's what I did. For twenty years, I was the boss, and my firm was successful, growing to thirty people at one point with clients worldwide.

Like most things, the firm was a success primarily because of hard work, good timing, and luck. Another contributing factor was that I lived in Vancouver, Canada, which was (and remains) the uncontested world capital of slick condominium sales and marketing. Fortunately, this was my firm's area of expertise.

We helped large developers entice buyers to buy in one condominium tower instead of another. We studied product differentiation at a microscopic level to find something that would make each condo tower seem different from the one next door.

"If we threw some Louis Vuitton throw cushions on the sofa in the display home, would that increase the velocity of sales?" "Would a closet that was really a secret door to a wine cellar make our homes more motivating?" "Should the sink in the master bathroom be flush with the counter, or sit on top of the counter like a pudding bowl?" These were real conversations. There are so many condominiums for sale in Vancouver that no angle was, or is, left unexplored.

As part of my job, I traveled to a lot of cities. We worked in a few cool places and, truth be told, a couple of ghastly ones too. I made a bit of money. I met fascinating people, and mostly it was fun.

To promote my company, I would commission research on topics that I was curious about and that I knew my clients were curious about too. Then, I'd write a book about the research and give speeches at industry conferences and conventions. It worked like a charm. You need to know this because it is pivotal to what happened next.

One day, I decided to sell my company and become a solo entrepreneur again. I had visions of a small consulting practice. I'd spend my days in my Saarinen Womb Chair with my feet propped up on the ottoman while taking important calls on a B&O headset. I'd kick my coffee addiction and instead learn to drink complicated teas.

I imagined jotting quick notes with an impressive fountain pen on deckle-edged ecru note cards until a reassuring soft chime emanating from some digital device signaled it was time to saunter off to the gym to meet my trainer or to a nearby cafe for a client lunch.

I also thought it might be smart to write another book. It had worked so well as a promotional strategy for my previous company. Why not carry on and do it again? Besides, it would lead to giving speeches, and I am one of those rare mutant-humans who loves public speaking.

As soon as I set my mind to the idea of a new book, two things collided in my brain, and a book idea was born.

The first thing was that my previous book *The Stackable Boomer* examined the tsunami of retiring baby boomers selling the family home in the suburbs and moving to condominiums. For that book, I commissioned a survey of one thousand baby boomers who had recently made this big move. I asked them questions about how their newly stacked lifestyle was working out. Consequently, I had a lot of information in my head about baby boomers.

The second thing was the deluge of stories and reports I was reading about how millennials were an entirely new species of human, unlike any that had ever come before. According to all this information, millennials required new workplaces, new human resource policies, and new kinds of products, services, and brands. We had to remake the world for millennials if all these stories were true.

But so many things I was reading about millennials seemed to match exactly what my research had uncovered about baby boomers. These similarities seemed like a coincidence at first, but the overlapping information kept popping up everywhere.

I remember the day the cartoon light bulb in my brain switched on.

I was in a cafe in Gastown, an area of Vancouver with one of the world's largest concentrations of millennials per square foot. While toying absentmindedly with a green tea matcha smoothie, I flipped to a story in the Sunday *New York Times* about how millennials really enjoyed woodworking and were renting table saws from tool-lending libraries in Brooklyn. It seems they liked making end tables and bookcases. This sounded exactly like the baby boomer men I'd spoken with for my last book who'd lamented the loss of the workshop bench in their suburban garage.

The article went on to say that millennial women liked gardening, baking, making pickles, and knitting. These were the same interests and hobbies I had heard the baby boomer women talking about.

Click went the light bulb. I knew what I wanted to write a book about. The boomers and millennials weren't as different from each other as the media would like us to believe. I put down my tea and used my iPhone to send an email to Kalym.

Kalym is a sociologist with ten years of research experience who is working on his PhD at a university in New Zealand. We had met a few years before through a website that connects freelancers with those who need to hire them. Our working relationship morphed into a long-distance friendship while working on my previous book because we were both willing to learn something new. I had to learn to speak *sociology*, which I swear on a stack of ancient scrolls is as challenging as learning fourteenth-century Latin. And Kalym had to learn to think like a marketer, which he did with a minimum of grumbling.

In subsequent emails and phone calls, I explained my idea for a book and commissioned him to do a study. I wanted to know if different generations were actually more similar than we thought. I knew the results of this study would be of great interest to my real estate developer clients, because if my hunch was right, it would help them build better condominium towers for people of all ages.

All the developers I know agree that diverse neighborhoods are happier places to live and work. But oddly, the prevailing strategy in the industry is to build condo towers for people who are more or less the same age, which is exactly the opposite of diverse. For boomers, we build buildings with chandeliers and marble bathrooms. For millennials, we build buildings with microsuites and coworking spaces.

But if I could prove that different generations of people all wanted the same things, then why couldn't diversity swoop through the front door and through the lobby, whoosh up the elevator, and spread out onto every floor? Why couldn't we build buildings for people of all ages to call home?

I was so convinced the research would come back and prove my theory to be true that I already had a snappy title for the book I was going to write: *The Boomerennials*.

I still love that title, and I still own the URL and might do something with it. Because, you see, despite all the effort it took to launch and analyze that study, the book was never written. Let me tell you why.

When I sat down and looked at *The Boomerennials* research results, a few things became abundantly clear. The data showed that we absolutely could build buildings for both millennials and baby boomers to live in. So that was great news.

Even better, people of all ages told us *they would pay a premium price*—as much as 15 percent more on average— to live in these diverse vertical villages. No one wanted to live in a building full of people all the same age. They told us that sounded boring.

But there was one condition. People were *only* willing to pay more for a condo or apartment if their neighbors *shared the same values* as they did.

This was a significant discovery. We tried to find other research that had looked into the same topic, but we couldn't find any. As far as we could tell, no one else had looked at the conditions required to make mixed-age buildings desirable. So it was settled. I was going to write *The Boomerennials* and start giving speeches.

But then I got to thinking.

I had been marketing condos for over a decade, so I knew that buying a home was the most meaningful and expensive purchase most people would ever make. I was well aware this was a complex decision fraught with emotions and issues about family, status, belonging, and more. Buying a home is a virtual stress-fest of the highest order.

And we'd just proven that even under these extreme circumstances, values determined what people would do. Age had nothing to do with how people behaved.

That's when I realized this discovery didn't have to be solely about condos.

If values are more important than age during times of peak stress, then why would it be any different when buying artichoke hearts or a pair of rubber boots? If values were so powerful, surely we could use them to profile audiences and predict behavior for everything, not just for condos.

So we built an enormous database of shared values.

This time we surveyed enough people to accurately profile the shared values of a target audience for any product, service, or brand in Canada or the United States.

And that's how Valuegraphics, the world's largest purpose-built database of shared values, was born.

THE AGE
OF AGE
IS OVER

VALUES ARE THE NEW BLACK

We're living through this fascinating moment in history in which there's a renaissance of interest in our shared values: the things that make us human.

There are scores of books being written about values, joining scores of others launched last year. There are books about how to find your values, and once you've found them, how to use them. Other books are about living a values-centric life, instilling our values in our children, creating values-focused companies, and understanding our brand values better.

Companies are hiring consultants to help them define their organizational values. You could choose to attend a conference somewhere different every week about using values to help you or your organization prosper.

So what if, instead of sitting in boardrooms saying, "We're making this for people who are this age and people who are that age," we said, "We're making this for people who value X and people who value Y?"

What if *what we valued* was the lens we looked through to create all the products, services, and brands that need creating?

It's impossible to predict what the result of a change like that would be. I am quite certain, however, the world would be a different place than it is right now. Why? Because what we value determines what we do.

THREE FRIENDS IN AN ALLEY AT MIDNIGHT

Three friends left a bar at midnight. Let's call them Dana, Kyle, and David.

They haven't seen each other for a long time. Consequently, they had been doing a lot of catching up that night, and they'd all had their last drink several drinks ago. They kept talking and laughing as they stumbled down the street, until they turned a corner and suddenly stopped.

In front of them was a dark alley.

It was so dark, in fact, they couldn't see down the alley at all even with the flashlight app on Dana's iPhone.

Now before we go any further, the thing you need to know about David is that his primary value is adventure. He always wants to try things that no one has tried before, and he loves extreme sports, like river kayaking in the mountains. David immediately wanted to go down that alley. He thought to himself, "Cool. That alley looks dangerous and exciting." He wanted to go down that alley very much.

But Kyle? His primary value has always been safety. He doesn't like risks of any kind, large or small. He thought to himself, "I'm not going down that alley. No damn way. That's a big, dark, scary alley. Are you insane? We just left the bar! We're drunk! We'd be crazy to go down a random dark alley at this time of night."

Then there's Dana. Her primary value is friendship. She doesn't care whether they go down the alley or not, as long as they stick together. She wants the three of them to do whatever they are going to do as a group; that's really her only concern.

The reaction these three friends have to that alley is a simple way to demonstrate how powerful values are. It's the same alley. The same night. But different values motivate different people to do different things.

Now, let's say your job is to convince a lot of people to visit that alley. One group of people you could try to convince are the people like David who value adventure. You might say something like this:

"This is the most exciting alley in the world! Never before has there been an alley packed with so many surprises! This is not an alley for the faint of heart!"

But for Kyle and other safety-first folks like him, that dark alley will probably be a bit more difficult to sell unless you said something like this:

> "Don't worry. This alley is extremely peaceful. We've dimmed the harsh lights. There are highly trained safety ambassadors who will greet you and guide you personally through this alley to your destination."

Or if you wanted to attract more people like Dana, for whom friendship is the filter for all decisions, you could say something like this:

> "This is the alley of friendship. Bring your friends to the alley, and your bond will be boosted to last-week-of-summer-camp level, the most intense friendship level of all."

The point is that you can tell a story about that alley in three different ways to appeal to the shared values of three different target audiences.

Even better, what if you knew about those three values before you built the alley? If you did, you could make decisions about location, lighting, design, and other aspects of the alley experience specifically to appeal to the values of the group you liked best. You might even decide to ignore one or more of these groups and focus on one profile that offered the best chance of success.

Those adventure hunters like David? Seems to me they'd be the easiest group to build a dark alley for.

Don't you agree?

THE MISSING LINK

Valuegraphics are the missing link of audience profiling tools. This all starts to sound a little manipulative, but in the business world, we have largely come to terms with the idea that we manipulate people. We call it *influencing* because it feels less Machiavellian that way.

We've been using demographics to define and attempt to influence target audiences for thousands of years. And in some ways, demographics are still very necessary. You still need to know that the people most likely to buy your teacups, T-shirts, tablets, or townhomes are rich or poor, young or old, male or female, and so on. But all demographics do is describe who your audience is. Demographics don't tell you what they care about or what motivates them, and that's really the problem. We have convinced ourselves that a simple description of a group of people is enough to start declaring what will make them do the things we want them to do. Which is false.

Psychographics were a big step forward, sort of. The term is often used to describe the behavior of a defined population, a kind of glance in the rearview mirror to see what the people you are trying to influence did yesterday or the year before or in the last buying cycle. This is interesting to know, but it's not predictive.

Some definitions of psychographics go on to embrace the idea that the term also includes the motivations, attitudes, and lifestyles of a target audience, but the proponents of this definition quickly point out that this information is hard to get your hands on unless people agree to fill out a survey.

And that's where Valuegraphics steps in.

Thanks to big data and contemporary survey collection methodologies, 75,000 people and counting have already completed our surveys. They've told us what they value—what they want, need, and expect from life. Using this data, we can extrapolate the shared values for a very precise target audience for a very specific product, service, or brand. And because what we value determines what we do, Valuegraphics Profiles allow any organization to motivate a group of people more readily, and be more influential, than ever before.

Think of it this way: demographics describe, and psychographics record, but Valuegraphics motivate.

VALUES
ARE
AGELESS

YOU ARE SITTING IN A BUBBLE BATH

Valuegraphics is an enormous and complex sociological database. As we've said, it contains the responses to as many as 340 questions from 75,000 surveys, and the number of respondents continues to grow. Trying to describe the Valuegraphics Database is very difficult unless you have an advanced degree in sociology and understand things like continuous dimensions, cultural cognition, and something called fuzzy data.

Which I don't. At least not very well. But I do understand bubble baths.

Imagine yourself sitting in a big, frothy bubble bath like an ancient god looking out over the bubble-based world in front of you. Every bubble in the bathtub is a Valuegraphics data point, and you are looking to see the patterns, how the data tends to clump together and form peaks in some areas and disperses to form valleys in others.

There are short mountains and tall mountains. Some have a broad base, and others are more like spires. The valleys come in all shapes and sizes too. The more you look, the more you see infinite types of mountains, hills, valleys, and plains, all made up of bubbles.

To make Valuegraphics easier to talk about, I decided to identify and focus on the top ten spires of data, what you might call the Himalayas of the bubble-bath landscape. I named each of these ten spires after the powerful *variable* at its core.

These ten variables attract data points like a magnet. The stronger the variable, the more data is drawn toward it, and the bigger the spire becomes. We call these ten biggest, most influential data spires the Valuegraphics Archetypes.

People who identify with one of these ten variables agree with everyone else who identifies with that variable about most things in life, pretty much all the time. Stop here for a moment and read that last sentence again. This is perhaps the most important finding from all the work we've done. Not only are there ten spires of data formed around ten key variables, but all the people in each of those ten groups agree on pretty much everything else, pretty much all the time. These are tribes. Tribes of like-minded people who can be identified because of one key variable that they share, instead of outdated age-based demographic tribes, who agree on hardly anything, ever.

MEET THE VALUEGRAPHICS ARCHETYPES

→ **The Adventure Club** are the funsters, the curious ones, always restless and looking to try new things, eat at new places, and meet new people.

→ **The Home Hunters Union** don't feel as much at home as they'd like, in all kinds of ways. They are unsettled, you might say.

→ **The Anti-Materialists Guild** are not into having stuff, owning stuff, or collecting stuff. None of that. Personally, I would not have much in common with these people at all.

→ **The Loyalist Lodge** members have had the same job forever and are loyal to a fault in all aspects of life. There are far more of these people than you might expect.

→ **The House of Creativity** believe they are creative, which could mean anything from occasional knitting to full-time interpretive dance.

→ **The Environmental Assembly** are focused on the planet. Mother Earth is in trouble, so we should buy the right detergents. And, kidding aside, do more serious things too.

→ **The Technology Fellowship** were deemed a fellowship because they all connect and relate to the world, and each other, through technology. They congregate virtually.

→ **The League of Workaholics** report being happy with eighty-hour workweeks, and they love the status and recognition they can buy as a result of all that hard work.

→ **The Savers Society** includes my mother-in-law, who will drive forty-five minutes across town because butter is on sale. She also likes to save animals, people, and little hotel soaps.

→ **The Royal Order of the Overdrawn** boasts both millionaires and grocery clerks as members: people who are always a few dollars shy of where they should be.

ARCHETYPES
IN ACTION

CHURCH PICNICS FOR COLLECTORS

Let's take a closer look at the Valuegraphics Archetype called the Loyalists Lodge. When people indicate that loyalty is the most important thing in their lives, they tend to agree with everyone else who says the same thing, 83 percent of the time.

Eighty-three percent is a lot of agreement. And since the Loyalists Lodge represents 17 percent of the total population, there are tens of millions of people who fit into this archetype.

Now imagine a small chain of ten community banks scattered around the midwestern United States who want to sign up new savings account customers. And let's say we were able to analyze their target audience and spot a significant number of people who belonged to the Loyalist Lodge archetype.

Here are three sample Valuegraphics facts we know about Loyalist Lodge members:

→ They are very likely to be religious.
→ They have a collection. It could be baseball cards, art, or any number of things.
→ They crave a sense of belonging.

That chain of midwestern banks could use those three simple Valuegraphics data points to brainstorm ideas like these:

→ Offer new savings account customers (and perhaps existing ones too) the opportunity to donate 0.25 percent interest on their account balance to the religious organization of their choice and match that amount.
→ Supply churches with a picnic supply basket, available free from the bank branch nearest you. Each basket contains paper cups, napkins, paper plates, cutlery, decorations, and all the other things a church group needs for a picnic. Of course, all those items would advertise the matching interest-rate donation savings account and point out how it benefits the church.
→ Collectors need places to keep their collections, so the bank could develop a new kind of safety deposit box

room, where collections of all kinds could be kept in a climate-controlled, fireproof environment.

→ And of course, in a three-way grand slam of Valuegraphics data leveraging, that bank could provide the desired sense of belonging by hosting collectors at meet-up picnics on the lawns of local churches, with bank employees on hand to sign up new savings account customers on the spot.

By focusing on the information in the Valuegraphics Profile of the target audience, the marketing team at this bank would be able to come up with interesting strategies and tactics. They also wouldn't waste a lot of time talking about ideas that were not part of the Valuegraphics Profile. By using big data to reduce the universe of possible responses, Valuegraphics makes innovative thinking less risky.

Before Valuegraphics, that same chain of banks would have analyzed their customers and decided, somehow, which age group was most likely to want savings accounts. Then they would have used age-based stereotypes to figure out ways to reach them.

But, millennials don't want savings accounts any more or less than baby boomers do. Offering free facial hair shampoo, avocado slicers, or Netflix accounts wouldn't make millennials any more or less likely to sign up for a new account than anyone of any age.

In fact, it turns out that age-based stereotypes are an

ill-advised strategy for profiling any audience. Some of the weakest variables in the Valuegraphics Database, where very few people agree about anything, are the variables based on age:

→ Baby boomers only agree on anything 13 percent of the time.
→ Millennials agree on things 15 percent of the time.
→ Generation X whimpers along, managing to agree a mere 11 percent of the time.

The Valuegraphics Database proves that people of the same age do not agree about much, ever. Yet we still keep using age to make decisions about how to spend our organizational time and money. And that's why this book needs to exist.

What we value, what makes us human, is how we decide what actions we will take today and tomorrow. If we can start planning, building, and designing a world for people with shared values instead of shared birthdays, we will all end up agreeing far more on everything than we do today. That sounds like a better world to me.

SHIRTS THAT SCREAM SUCCESS

You wake up one morning and discover that, magically, you are now a menswear manufacturer with a reputation for making men's casual shirts. It's your job to create a new shirt brand today, and you need to make a few decisions.

The Biggest Fake News of Our Time

All those stories you've been reading about how we must change the world for millennials? You can ignore them. Millennials are not a thing. How can we make decisions about changing anything to suit a group of people who don't agree with each other and have nothing important in common except the year in which they were born?

Imagine a target audience of forty-six-year-old men with white-collar jobs. They are married, and they make $200,000 a year. That's a fairly concise demographic description of a desirable audience for men's casual shirts. Can you launch a new brand based on this information? I can pretty much guarantee that someone somewhere today is tackling this issue. Let's think about what the options might be.

Forty-six-year-old, white-collar men making $200K must be working in an office, so they are probably in suits all week. On the weekend, they like to have fun, so you could logically propose a new line of shirts called Antidote in colors that are an antidote to traditional office palettes of blue or white. Antidote shirts will be brightly colored and feature fairly aggressive but masculine patterns. The weekends are when these deskbound executives are permitted to ditch the work uniform and really express their personality that the corporate dress code requires them to keep under wraps all week.

Alternatively, you could launch a line of shirts called FormFunction. This line of shirts is made with technical fabrics, and they're designed to resemble classic menswear staples. Customers can choose between a golf shirt, a button-down, a T-shirt, and a sweatshirt. They are available in solid blue, grey, or white, so they pretty much match anything already in the customer's closet. What makes the FormFunction line interesting is that these shirts are designed to go from the gym, to brunch, to the grocery store, and finally the backyard barbecue without needing to be changed out. That's because the fabric actually kills the bacteria that makes sweat stink. Forty-six-year-old, white-collar guys don't want to be changing shirts all day long on the weekend. They don't want to think about what they are wearing on the weekend at all. They want to grab something and go. Guys hate all that fussing around with clothes.

Those are both great ideas. But you know what else you could do? About a hundred other things, many of which would be good ideas too. However, each idea would be open for debate by NSIAC, the New Shirt Idea Approval Committee. It takes a half dozen meetings, normally, to convince the committee members from design, purchasing, manufacturing, sales, marketing, and distribution to green-light an idea. Tempers flare. Internal office politics play a large role in the decision, of course. And it's not always the best ideas that live to see the light of day.

But what if you knew the Valuegraphics for your audience? As a hypothetical example, let's say the vast majority of your audience fit into our Valuegraphics Archetype called the League of Workaholics.

We know all kinds of things about the League of Workaholics, but let's focus on these three:

→ They are very materialistic.
→ They work eighty hours a week or more.
→ They like awards and recognition, and they light up like a Christmas tree when they are praised for their success.

Given those three Valuegraphics data points about our audience, I have a proposal for the NSIAC to consider. I'd suggest launching a line of shirts called Golden Truth, made of the most expensive cotton-linen blends in the world and priced twice as high as any other shirt available on the market today. The craftsmanship needs to be exceptional, as these are more than shirts: these are status symbols meant to communicate the success of the wearer. To justify the price, each shirt comes in its own monogrammed shirt box made of cedar, and a line of text is embroidered on the right shirt cuff, just above the edge—discreet enough that it doesn't feel flashy, but it's there if you look for it.

That line of text on the cuff is personalized for each customer (these shirts are not off the rack; they must be made to measure) and features a favorite motto or saying of the shirt wearer—his own Golden Truth. These lines of text are embroidered with real gold thread, of course, so the customized feature of the shirt is quite literally jewelry that memorializes the words of wisdom of the man wearing the garment.

I bet the approval committee would green-light that idea pretty fast. They couldn't argue with the logic of the strategy because the idea is directly linked to statistically accurate data about what that customer values.

The bottom line here is that we should not be making assumptions about any target audience based on how old they are, how much they earn, or anything else except their values. It really doesn't work, and it wastes precious time and money.

The first two shirt ideas, Antidote and FormFunction, might be successful, and they might not. But as soon as we know the Valuegraphics of our shirt buyer, the third idea, Golden Truth...well, it becomes a pretty safe bet that those shirts are destined to become highly sought after by the target audience they were created for.

THE FORTY VALUES OF VALUEGRAPHICS

You already know we discovered Valuegraphics thanks to an original batch of 40,000 surveys, and as many as 340 questions. You also know the database continues to grow, and we're at 75,000 surveys today. By the time you read this, the number of survey respondents could easily have doubled. No matter how you slice it, Valuegraphics is based on an enormous amount of compiled data, and it keeps getting more enormous every time we use it.

But what were all those questions about? What does the database reveal about the values of a target audience? I'm glad you asked.

There are forty different values represented in the Valuegraphics Database that together summarize the amazing complexity of what it means to be human. They are ranked in the list that follows according to popularity with our respondents.

We ended up asking 340 questions in these surveys. Why? Because in each of ten different thematically constructed surveys, we asked respondents to rank the values according to how important they were to them personally. We then asked them to rate the importance of each value to their family life overall and their level of satisfaction with the value on the day of completing the survey. We also asked them to choose the values they would most like to work on and improve, and to identify the core values they would go to extremes to ensure they didn't have to live without. We then went on a question-asking spree about the values they had indicated were most important to them. For example, if someone said creativity was a core value, we asked them to define what creativity means to them and how they go about meeting their needs around that value, and so on.

It's interesting that the top three, most-motivating values are all about membership in a collective in one way or another. This means *belonging* is a kind of metavalue. It turns out that belonging is the key to pretty much everything in our lives and in our world. We want it, we crave more of it, and we will do anything required to find as much of it as we can. There's your hint of hope for the future of mankind.

Here are the forty values contained in the Valuegraphics Database, ranked in order of popularity.

1. Belonging
2. Family
3. Relationships
4. Health/Well-Being
5. Personal Growth
6. Ability to Meet Basic Needs
7. Employment Security
8. Religion/Spirituality
9. Financial Security
10. Material Possessions
11. Security
12. Community
13. Creativity and Imagination
14. Personal Responsibility
15. Inner Harmony
16. Experiences
17. Compassion
18. Equality
19. Freedom of Speech
20. Love
21. Wealth
22. Happiness
23. Trustworthiness
24. Authority
25. Ambition
26. Money
27. Friendships
28. Peace
29. Self-Expression
30. Leisure
31. Social Standing
32. Politeness
33. Intimacy
34. Political Freedom
35. Tolerance
36. Unselfishness
37. Self-Control
38. Independence
39. Influence
40. Determination

WHAT WE VALUE DETERMINES WHAT WE DO

DO-IT-YOURSELF VALUEGRAPHICS

Using the Valuegraphics Database, we can customize very precise Valuegraphics Profiles for a specific industry, or even for a single product, service, or brand. Some examples of these insights taken from Custom Valuegraphics Profiles are included in subsequent sections of this book.

But to get you started on your own thinking about the shared values of your target audiences, I've included a short survey as an appendix. It's called the DIY Valuegraphics Archetype Ranking Tool.

Using the ranking tool will help you understand which of the ten Valuegraphics Archetypes are most prevalent in your target audience. Once you know that, the corresponding starter packs will help you boost the effectiveness of your product development, design, marketing, sales, human resources, internal culture, and more.

Each starter pack is a scrapbook of cues, clues, and ideas for one of the top ten most powerful Valuegraphics Archetypes.

It's vital to note this is not meant to replace a Custom Valuegraphics Profile.

Think about a room filled with one thousand people. Now ask two different friends to go into that room and come back with a description of the crowd they encountered. You will receive two entirely different descriptions.

Each of your two friends will have lived a different life, know different things, and have different areas of expertise. So, of course, they will describe the same group of people in two different ways.

What's interesting is the description you form of the group of people in that room will be far more accurate if your friends compare notes and agree on a collaborative interpretation. If you have ten friends do the same thing, your final description would be even more true. The point is that interpretation is a very important part of the Valuegraphics profiling methodology.

Furthermore, to be statistically accurate, we must look at all the relevant data that could apply in a particular scenario.

Imagine if you sent your friends into that room of 1,000 people and asked them, once again, to describe the group. But this time, you only allowed them to see 10 of the 1,000 people. Or they were only allowed to look at everyone's shoes. Or they were only permitted to look at the people standing right in the very center of the room, or just the people in each corner.

In every case, it's a start, and it's better than not being able to see anything at all. At least you have some information about the people in the room and not about random other people who are nowhere near that room.

But it's not the statistically accurate custom report you could receive if all the possible data were analyzed and if the right group of individuals were asked to collaborate on interpreting the findings.

So why do this exercise at all?

Because, as I've already pointed out, at least it's a start. That's why the ten starter packs that follow are called starter packs. The information you will have to work with once you use the Archetype Ranking Tool, and the clues in the starter packs, will be far superior to the information you'd have about the people in that room if neither you nor your friends were allowed to set foot in that room at all.

Describing the group in that room without being allowed to see them at all would be absurd. Surely no one would do that? It would just be taking a wild guess at who might be in that room and pretending to know something about them because you'd once seen some people in a similar room somewhere else a long time ago. That would be like, well, using the demographic stereotypes still used in boardrooms all over the world today.

DIY VALUEGRAPHICS STEP ONE

Since Valuegraphics is about profiling groups of people, first, you'll need to define the parameters of the group. Who is in the room you want to profile? Figuring that out is step one.

There are many things you could do. Maybe you want to understand how the archetypes rank with your current customers. If that's the case, you can simply send out the ranking tool to your customer database.

If you don't have a customer database, you could simply ask for some basic demographic information—starting today—each time your organization has an interaction with a customer or client.

You might also consider administering the ranking tool to your staff. Or the people in your neighborhood. Or everyone who comes to a special event. The possibilities are only limited by your imagination.

As long as you are asking the ten questions about values on the ranking tool, you may as well ask a few demographic questions about age, gender, and income too. It's always good to know the demographics of your audience, as well as the Valuegraphics that will help you motivate them more.

Once you have the responses from your target audience, you simply add up the results and find out which archetypes are most prevalent. It's also a good idea to note which archetypes are the least prevalent. More perspective is always better.

There will inevitably be leaps of faith required once you start to analyze your results. Remember, all you are trying to do is rank which Valuegraphics Archetypes you have more of and which ones are less represented. This is not simply about picking the top-ranked archetype and calling it a day. Unfortunately, it's not that simple.

Now, let's turn to the starter packs in the chapters that follow.

DIY VALUEGRAPHICS STEP TWO

Once you have the Valuegraphics Archetype rankings for your target audience, review the information in the corresponding starter packs from the following pages. You'll immediately begin to understand your target audience better because you'll know more about what they value, and what they value determines what they do.

A simple brainstorming session with the appropriate people from your organization should be next. You might even invite a few members of your target audience to join you around the boardroom table.

We've been using age-based profiles, however flawed, to do this for decades now. So you are familiar with the mechanics of using audience profiles to guide a brainstorming session. This is no different, except the profiles you are starting with are based on fact, not fiction.

If I led you to a kitchen counter on which sat mixing bowls, flour, eggs, sugar, cream, oranges, and cream cheese, you may not know exactly what you are going to make with these ingredients, but you know it's *not* a roast beef dinner with Yorkshire pudding and mashed yams. You'd immediately start trying different ways and methods to make a creamy, citrusy cake-torte-confection-thingy that tasted great.

DEFINITIONS YOU WILL FIND USEFUL

While working with the Valuegraphics starter packs, here are some terms and definitions you will find useful:

Core Values are the beliefs we hold closest to our hearts, the things that motivate us the most and, consciously or subconsciously, determine everything we do. When you can identify the core values of an entire group of people, you can motivate that audience in a powerful way.

Core values cut across age, income, and gender. They do not discriminate. Use the core values of your target audience to design products, services, brands, policies, and ideas, and you will motivate more people more often.

Certainties are the unassailable truths for the people within a Valuegraphics Archetype. Use these as mandatory filters to make decisions about all aspects of your product, service, brand, policy, or idea.

Likelihoods are those things that are not as widespread or deeply rooted as certainties but still stand out in the Valuegraphics data. Likelihoods should be thought of as contextual. They can help you design your product, service, or brand, but they are not essential. Sometimes it's nice to add an olive or lemon peel to a martini, but even with no garnish at all, you can still make a great martini.

THE ADVENTURE CLUB

AKA THE RESTLESS

→ 11% of the population
→ Agree on values 89% of the time

MEET JOSH

It was early Tuesday morning, and already Josh wasn't having a great day. He'd bought his plane ticket and emailed the registration forms for his seventh Yoga Bro four-day intensive in Arizona, which was only a month away. But he was short on his monthly budget as a result and would need to make it up from somewhere.

He would have to cut his expenses. But how? The phone bill wasn't even a consideration, so he would have to skip a Visa payment or cut back on food. He chose food.

He would eat at his girlfriend's place most of the time, he decided. Otherwise, he'd relive his childhood and eat ramen noodles. That's what his mom used to make when she was between gigs, which seemed to be most of the time.

A self-imposed food challenge would be good practice for the mandatory Yoga Bro fasting, he thought. The intense food restrictions over those four days in the desert were one of the toughest parts of the experience. "Be more with less." That was the Yoga Bro core philosophy. He'd considered having the line inked on his calf, but so far, he hadn't been brave enough. Instead, he bought a dog tag with the letters stamped on the surface. He wore it on a chain under his shirt to the office every day. It reminded him of what was really important.

Despite his excitement about his upcoming Yoga Bro adventure, his day was spiraling downward. His newish girlfriend, Daphne, had laid down the law while chewing aloe vera paste and quinoa flatbread in the kitchen.

"I think I've been very patient," she said, "but come on. Every night, you and your Yoga Bros are either at the gym, high on something, or you're dancing like idiots in a nightclub. And now, four solid days of this in the desert? I really don't see space for me in your life."

Josh had always disliked how Daphne talked while chewing her food. He listened to her ultimatum and watched tiny quinoa crumbs bounce across the white kitchen counter.

He knew in his heart how this movie would play out. He'd seen this film before. He'd come back from the desert, back to his job at the most boring logistics company in the world, and he'd break up with Daphne to avoid being dumped. There was only one thing left to do.

He grabbed her head tenderly with both hands, planted a big kiss on her forehead, and said, "I'm late for work." He grabbed his gym bag and walked out the front door.

ARCHETYPE OVERVIEW

Who doesn't love a good adventure? As it turns out, when you ask people directly, only 11 percent of the population would say they do. This makes the adventurous among us more of a rarity than one might expect.

The alternate name for this archetype is the Restless, because they are always looking for what could be new, better, and more exciting. The Adventure Club members would rather not eat in the same restaurant twice and would be unlikely to go to the same place on a vacation more than once either.

They'll be curious about everything and will adopt and discard new ideas and trends easily.

From big decisions to small ones, they are driven by a desire to try new things, to learn more, to meet more people, to have more experiences, to see more things, and to grow.

They are also heavily influenced by belonging. They like to be part of something bigger than themselves.

They are prime candidates for sports teams, fraternities/sororities, clubs, and the like. They probably travel in groups. They avoid being alone.

CORE VALUES

1. Personal Growth
2. Experiences
3. Belonging

CERTAINTIES

→ They have lived in as many as ten different places and as many as three different countries.

→ Their possessions are far less important than their experiences.

→ They would like to be financially secure but are not willing to make sacrifices.

→ They are more likely than average to be single.

→ They tend to be uninterested in politics.

LIKELIHOODS

→ They are foodies and enjoy new food experiences.

→ They regularly spend time at a gym or in fitness classes.

→ They are more likely than average to have used recreational drugs.

→ They will spend at least three nights per week out being social.

- → As many as half have never voted.
- → Approximately half come from a low-income background.
- → They are unlikely to think of themselves as religious, but they enjoy visiting places with religious significance.
- → They are unlikely to be concerned about their quality of life.

IN THEIR OWN WORDS: REAL QUOTES FROM REAL SURVEY RESPONDENTS

- → "I strive to be a better me every day, and that makes me a better me every day."
- → "We are shaped by who we spend time with."
- → "I enjoy pushing my limits and seeing where they really are."
- → "I don't assume my current way of living is the way I should be living."
- → "Do what you've always done, and you'll get what you've always got? No thanks!"
- → "Every barrier is another chance to grow."

HALL OF FAME

- → Indiana Jones
- → Richard Branson
- → Tough Mudder
- → Anthony Bourdain

- → Patagonia
- → Amelia Earhart
- → Bear Grylls
- → Christopher Columbus
- → Jeep
- → Tony Robbins

THE HOME HUNTERS UNION

AKA THE UNSETTLED

→ 37% of the population
→ Agree on values 85% of the time

MEET VAL

Every week, Valerie (Val to her friends) squirrels away a few grocery dollars to fund her scrapbooking hobby. When she steals a few hours alone, when Bill has backed the Honda out of the driveway and gone off to work in the taupe microfiber-lined office cubicle where he spends his days or when he's out at the football game for "cheers and beers," as he calls it, she works on her scrapbooks about places she wants to visit and maybe even live. She discovers these places on TV, on Facebook, or in the newspaper. Her inspirations are varied.

Exotic places figure prominently in her work. But, oddly enough, even more exciting for Val are the places that are not very different from where she lives now but somehow better. She goes to tourism centers for brochures about neighboring towns and cities, and she goes to open houses on the weekend to find inspiration about other ways of living.

It's not that she's unhappy. It's more that she's suspicious there might be an even happier life she could arrange for herself and her family. She's really not sure what it is, so she views her scrapbooking as a kind of happiness research.

She feels a bit guilty about using grocery dollars for scrapbooking supplies, especially when she thinks about the credit card debt, but it's the only thing that helps her cope with the anxiety she feels hanging over her, anxiety about the future. Surely scrapbooking is better than the Ativan prescription her friend Ramona relies on.

When Val is being creative, thinking about all the ways life could turn out to be more perfect, it helps her forget, even for a few moments or a half hour, even though there's absolutely nothing wrong with her life and she feels blessed to be safe and loved, she's afraid this might be as good as it ever gets.

ARCHETYPE OVERVIEW

The members of the Home Hunters Union are looking to *build a home,* which is not necessarily the same thing as wanting to *buy a home.* In fact, the other name we sometimes use for this Valuegraphics Archetype is the Unsettled.

While a high percentage of this very large group may actually move to a new home in the next two years, at this moment, it's only a possible solution they are considering because of the feeling of unsettledness that permeates their life. What they really are searching for is to *feel more at home.* A home is about life and family and about so much more than the four walls that surround you.

The Home Hunters represent a diverse group of folks from all different backgrounds, but they are still in alignment with each other's values 85 percent of the time. A lack of political interest, a preference for experiences instead of things, and an enjoyment of sports typifies the Valuegraphics of this archetype. But topping the list, whether a member is twenty-one or eighty-three, is that their family is their first priority.

I suspect this group is here to stay, and I expect the size of this group is a reflection of our times. The thing is, these people are unsettled, uncomfortable, and unsure about the future. No matter where you live in North America today, most would agree that our lives feel less stable than they did before. The members of the Home Hunters Union use these tumultuous times as an excuse to double-down on what they feel is most important. They are focused on protecting their own basic needs and those of their family. They want to experience the world in a more meaningful way.

CORE VALUES

1. Meeting Basic Needs
2. Experiences

CERTAINTIES

→ They are more likely than average to be currently renting their home.
→ They are interested in unconventional living environments and have an open mind about what a home could be.
→ They are attracted to unique and interesting features in a home.
→ They are unsettled and are open to alternative solutions.
→ They are uninterested in politics.

LIKELIHOODS

→ A full third of this group is carrying a major debt load.
→ Another third of the Home Hunters consider themselves to be creative, exhibiting crossover characteristics with another archetype: The House of Creativity.
→ Home Hunters have a number of shared characteris-

tics with the restless members of The Adventure Club archetype. Notably, they are the second most likely archetype to be attracted to experiences more than possessions.

→ They are very focused on meeting and protecting the basic needs of their family (food, clothing, shelter, school, job, etc.). Other comforts are less important.

→ They likely frequently feel anxious, insecure, and unsure.

→ Three-quarters of this group were born in North America.

→ An above-average number of this archetype are not educated beyond high school.

→ Almost half of this group have been fired from at least one job.

→ They are big sports fans, perhaps because connecting to other fans of a particular team creates a temporary sense of being more at home.

IN THEIR OWN WORDS: REAL QUOTES FROM REAL SURVEY RESPONDENTS

→ "I believe and accept that there are more important things in life than money."

→ "Ever since I was a kid, I've always valued doing something over getting something."

→ "Seeing how others live makes me more comfortable with my own struggles."

→ "I want to provide my children with the opportunities I never had."

→ "I try to live in the moment and not worry about the future."

→ "I'm happy where I am right now, but I'd like to try living in some other places too."

HALL OF FAME

→ Tim Taylor
→ Volvo
→ Nancy Botwin
→ Norman Rockwell
→ Costco
→ Johnson & Johnson
→ Nike

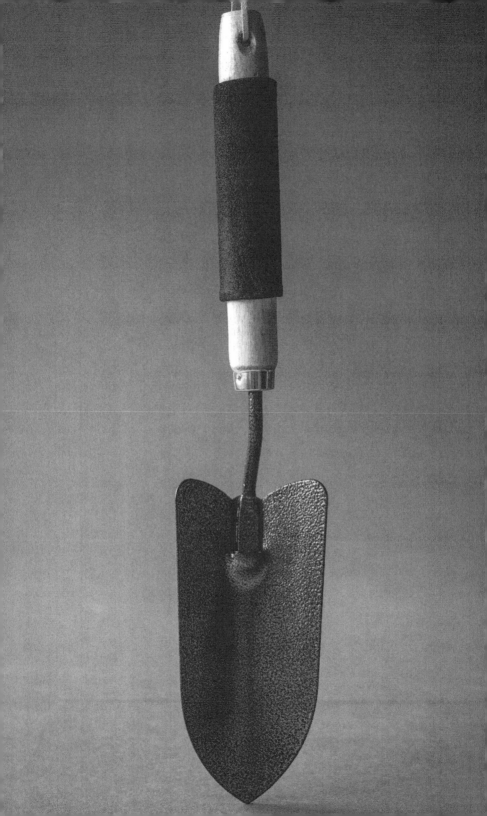

THE ANTI-MATERIALISTS GUILD

→ 13% of the population
→ Agree on values 85% of the time

MEET CATARINA

Catarina is a staff supervisor for three group homes for at-risk kids in the poorest parts of the city. She lives in the smallest apartment she could find so she can save as much money as possible as quickly as possible because she wants to buy a house and needs a down payment to do so.

Her apartment is so small she can walk across it diagonally from one corner to the next in six big strides. She had to do a lot of painting and other cosmetic work when she moved in, but she didn't mind that because the rent is ridiculously low, and the place suits her fine. It also means she doesn't need much furniture or all the other things her friends seem to be spending their money on all the time.

She loves gardening and volunteers at the community garden a few blocks from where she lives. She spends every moment she can kneeling on a plank over the dark soil with Signal, her skittish half-Australian Shepherd at her side. She sometimes spends whole weekends fussing about the rows of beans, tomatoes, carrots, and the acorn squash she loves to barbecue and baste with butter. She loves the hours out there in the sun, chatting with her neighbors, but one of the best perks is all the fresh produce she brings home. Vegetables that she helped plant, tend, and harvest taste better somehow. Often, she even has excess eggplants or snap peas she can't eat herself, so she bundles them up and drops them on the doorsteps of the seniors who live on her street. She likes doing nice things for people, and it makes her happier when she can.

Along with adopting a meatless diet, because "don't get her started on industrial farms," all those free fresh veggies are helping her save for the down payment that is central to her long-term home-ownership goals. One day, she wants a big garden of her very own.

ARCHETYPE OVERVIEW

The Anti-Materialists, as the name suggests, are the only Valuegraphics Archetype whose members are in agreement about being *against* something. These folks do not want more stuff, they are not motivated by stuff, and they find the idea of excess stuff to be wasteful. I bet they can even be a bit *judgy* about people who enjoy having a lot of material possessions. I don't mean they would be intentionally nasty, but they'd probably drop hints whenever the opportunity presented itself. "We have a car-share membership, but I can see where your collection of seven or is it eight vintage show cars must be, um, satisfying."

These folks are ultra-*belongy*. Their top values are all about bonding with and having an impact on other people. They'll be the ones volunteering at the school or community center or working long hours on a project associated with their cultural background or heritage. They are fascinated with where their family came from. Maybe they are arranging to teach younger people the craftwork of their ancestors or running a program that pairs seniors and children in the community to increase intergenerational understanding. They are probably always learning new things themselves too, either in formal settings or simply by being curious and researching the new things they encounter as they move through the world day by day.

This caring attitude extends to the animal kingdom, as they are likely to be vegetarians and eat a meatless diet for philosophical rather than health reasons. While it didn't come up in our data specifically, if they decide to have a pet, it would most certainly come from a shelter, or it would be a rescue animal that had been found living in distress.

They are going to be the last to buy a new iPhone or laptop because the one they have works just fine. It's wasteful to have a new piece of technology when there are so many older models filling up landfills. They might reconsider this stance on new technology if they knew of a charity or program that refurbished old phones for disadvantaged teens in hardscrabble parts of the world. After all, they aren't against tech, they simply don't feel the need to always have the newest version of everything that comes along. They believe they are too smart to fall for the pressure to constantly upgrade that "marketers have foisted on the world."

CORE VALUES

1. Family
2. Relationships
3. Community

CERTAINTIES

→ They place very little value on increasing material possessions.

→ They do not register possessions as an expectation, need, or want.

LIKELIHOODS

→ They have less of a history in North America than the other archetypes.

→ They are the most likely archetype to speak at least two languages.

→ They highly value creating new memories and keeping alive the stories of their ancestors.

→ They have the highest propensity, of all archetypes, to be vegetarians.

→ They are unlikely to be early adopters of new technology.

→ They place a high value on education, both formal and self-directed.

→ They care deeply about the environment.

IN THEIR OWN WORDS: REAL QUOTES FROM REAL SURVEY RESPONDENTS

→ "Family is the most important thing; it dictates all my decisions. My family is my life."

→ "If my community was threatened, I would stand up and fight. I've done it before and I'm ready to do it again and again in this messed-up world we're now in."

→ "Caring about those around me gives me value in my life."

→ "I want to reward my wife for the faith she has shown me all these years."

→ "I would like to give my kids the chance to do whatever they want in life, not just what they have to do."

→ "I want to show my sons there is more to life than iPads and Instagram."

HALL OF FAME

→ Gandhi
→ Mother Teresa
→ Car-Sharing Companies
→ Buy Nothing Day
→ Tom's Shoes
→ The Minimalists
→ Allen Ginsberg
→ Alice Waters

THE LOYALISTS LODGE

→ 17% of the population
→ Agree on values 83% of the time

MEET KEVIN

Kevin likes to think he's a spontaneous and contemporary fellow, but his friends all see the patterns that rule his life. He'll wear a pair of chinos or a shirt until it is frayed and worn, not because he can't afford to buy something new but because it gives him comfort to stick to the tried and true. Kevin has taken this trait to extremes at times, and he has learned to ignore the taunts and jeers of his friends who think he should update his look more often.

Kevin lives a life bound by an almost Samurai-warrior-like set of personal rules that he feels are essential to keep everything from spinning out of control. He works out at the gym religiously with a very set routine on very set days and a level of fitness dedication that some might see as fanatical. He is devoted to his wife and children, even though he's not entirely sure he is in love with his wife as much as he used to be. He works long hours and would sooner max out his credit cards than not meet his financial obligations to his staff and customers.

Kevin has worked so hard at times that he's brought himself to the brink of physical exhaustion. He has even taken quick naps under his desk so he could work all night and meet a customer deadline. He routinely says no to the things he *wants* to do with his time because he has things he feels he *must* do instead.

But Kevin is happy. He is self-aware. He laughs about his extreme behavior with his friends, and occasionally allows himself to bust loose and have a good time. When he does relax however, even then, it seems like he's only having fun because he knows he should.

ARCHETYPE OVERVIEW

We all know at least one person who is so loyal to a job, an idea, or a situation that it defies logic to everyone except the person in question. Sometimes it probably defies logic to that person too, and they can't quite place a finger on the reason for their loyalty, except that it feels like the right thing to do.

Family, relationships, and belonging are the core values that this group holds near and dear to their hearts. The primary anchor to those three values is, logically, a nearly impenetrable sense of loyalty. If they are on a team, they will give their last buck to any team member who needs it. They will do anything to help their friends. They are loyal to their family to a fault.

Recently, members of the Musqueam Indian Band in British Columbia, where I live, taught me that in their traditional language, there is no word for "friend" that doesn't also mean family. The Loyalists personify that powerful linguistic lesson.

Because they grew up going to church or temple, they have remained loyal to that practice, even if they don't fully believe in the religious aspects of the faith. They keep going out of a sense of loyalty and for the community they feel part of while there. Another way to look at loyalty is this: change of any kind is something these people would prefer to avoid.

They won't want to change habits, jobs, relationships, or ideas. In other words, they want their whole world to stay as loyal to the status quo as they are. The restaurant they always go to is the best one to go to again today, preferably to sit in the same booth as the last time and the time before that. The jeans they've been buying for twenty years are great. They don't need to try another brand. They vote for the same party, watch the same TV shows, and absorb information from trusted, reliable sources.

They also collect something. This makes perfect sense because, after all, what is collecting but a form of loyal fascination with a particular object or object category?

THE LOYALISTS LODGE CORE VALUES

1. Family
2. Relationships
3. Belonging

CERTAINTIES

→ They are likely to be religious.
→ They don't want things to change, and they certainly don't go looking for change.
→ They are likely to be married with children.
→ They are NOT attracted to chasing achievements of most kinds.

LIKELIHOODS

→ They are loyal to the company they work for and are eager to climb the ranks.
→ They love watching TV.
→ They vote and are, unsurprisingly, loyal to a favorite political party.
→ They believe in helping others and have an altruistic streak.

→ They are collectors: stamps, baseball cards, shoes—they are loyal to a collectible category.
→ They are sexually very conservative. We even had trouble getting responses to survey questions that strayed too close to this most personal of topics.

IN THEIR OWN WORDS: REAL QUOTES FROM REAL SURVEY RESPONDENTS

→ "Loyalty is a true test of character, especially in tough times. It gives me stability."
→ "How has family shaped who I am today? In every way possible."
→ "I love feeling the synergy of a team or group."
→ "A value isn't a value unless you stick to it in the tough times."
→ "People give up on their home lives too easily in the modern world."
→ "Hopefully, my team will win the Super Bowl."

HALL OF FAME

→ Forrest Gump
→ John Goodman
→ Tim Hortons
→ Budweiser
→ Blackberry
→ Hank Hill

→ Chevrolet

→ Apple

→ Star Trek

→ Lassie

THE HOUSE OF CREATIVITY

→ 35% of the population
→ Agree on values 82% of the time

MEET SYLVIA

Once a month, Sylvia goes to a naked yoga class at a yoga studio an hour away from where she lives. She drives the hour each way so she can be at least somewhat anonymous. Figuring out why she has hang-ups about nudity is kind of her obsession, and it's one of the main reasons she keeps going back. She is quite open about going to Wreck Beach, the local nudist sunbathing mecca, on hot summer weekends, so nudity doesn't always bother her. But naked yoga feels outside the boundaries of respectable behavior, which both excites and confounds her. She wants to be more open-minded. She doesn't want this to bother her so much.

Sylvia is extremely proud that her paintings have started to sell for enough money that she can afford to be a full-time painter. Even more, she is thrilled she can stop working part-time at the company her husband founded. Even though the company has paid the bills for all their married life, it was stifling for her to spend time there, and it took her hours to get back into her painting-brain after she'd finished a shift. She has no idea how people can spend forty, fifty, or sixty hours a week working for someone else, being told what to do. She believes in listening to the right side of her brain and letting her art call the shots, which is so much more rewarding. "Oh, well," she thinks to herself. "I am so lucky I can do what I want to do. Yay me."

Sylvia sells her paintings to people who wander into her studio on a popular tourist street. Frankly, the rent she pays is exorbitant, and she doesn't quite break even every month. But she needs to be there instead of working out of a more affordable but deserted studio in some other part of town. It feeds her soul being around all that bustling energy, and she truly believes that things will pick up. She's talking to hotels about making art for their guest rooms, and frequently, she is asked to reproduce one of her paintings in a different size and with "a bit more blue" or "less green" so it will fit into someone's life or interior design more perfectly. She charges more for custom work, so she's always happy to oblige.

ARCHETYPE OVERVIEW

The Creatives constitute a unique archetype because of the way they live their lives wrapped up with their own thoughts. If you scan the list of values, certainties, and likelihoods that follow, you'll note that most are about their inner life and how they feel about it. Since being creative is a core value, they will respond well to anything that reinforces their own sense of creativity.

In our surveys, we didn't define what we meant when we asked about creativity. As long as respondents thought of themselves as creative and spent at least five hours a week doing that creative thing, they were included in this archetype. Belonging and family are core values too, but when compared to the rest of the characteristics of this group, they are almost there as an afterthought. You can imagine the thought bubble over their head as they filled out the survey, "Well, of course, I care about belonging and family, but that's enough about that. I have a lot more to say about me."

They report being frustrated with boredom, and they love having a million projects on the go. This is very likely because they are self-employed or working multiple jobs. After all, doing what someone else wants you to do all day long is the ultimate version of boredom for someone who is mentally occupied doing a million creative things at once.

When you are creative, and you see something you think should be yours, you rationalize the acquisition quite easily. Consequently, these people are in debt so frequently it's become normal, and they are not worried about it.

They are in touch with their emotions and have to remind themselves not to be too emotionally forthcoming around people who find emotions more difficult to discuss. They love their kids, if they have any, but don't actively parent like they know they should. They think children should be more responsible for themselves anyway. Despite this lack of parenting guilt, they probably have surrogate children in the form of younger friends who they find more creatively intriguing than people of their own age.

Sports, as far as they are concerned, are a huge waste of time and energy and couldn't be more uninteresting.

They are quite open to trying new things in many different forms, even those that others may consider taboo. After all, the very definition of creativity is to question conventional thinking.

CORE VALUES

1. Being Creative
2. Belonging
3. Family

CERTAINTIES

→ They spend five or more hours per week doing something they consider creative.

→ They are frustrated with boredom.

→ They are likely to be self-employed, or they work multiple jobs.

LIKELIHOODS

→ They are likely to be in debt.

→ They are highly emotionally aware.

→ They are the most sexually open of the archetypes.

→ They aren't likely to be actively involved in their children's lives, if they have children.

→ They aren't interested in mainstream sports.

→ They are somewhat likely to feel unsettled.

→ They are likely to consider mainstream employment to be both boring and beneath them.

IN THEIR OWN WORDS: REAL QUOTES FROM REAL SURVEY RESPONDENTS

→ "Being creative gives me opportunities to express and explore who I am."

→ "By searching for ways to belong, I got in touch with why I wanted to belong."

→ "By sharing everything about myself with my family and friends, I have been humbled."

→ "My creativity is my therapy. Painting calms me."
→ "I want to make others feel welcome to join my creative friends. But some people find self-expression intimidating, I guess."
→ "I could do a better job helping out raising the kids. I don't do enough there."

HALL OF FAME

→ Leonardo Da Vinci
→ Tesla
→ Vice
→ Albert Einstein
→ Pablo Picasso
→ Virgin
→ Frank Lloyd Wright
→ Pinterest

THE ENVIRONMENTAL ASSEMBLY

→ 17% of the population

→ Agree on values 82% of the time

MEET JOHN

John works as a development manager at a large real estate development company. While sometimes his career feels at odds with his growing concern for the environment, because of his seniority in the firm, he is able to impact the green agenda internally in a significant way. So he stays. "New buildings will be built with or without me. At least if I am on the inside, I can make more environmentally friendly buildings." He sees himself as a kind of white-collar warrior for Mother Earth.

At home, he is constantly upset with his wife, Glenna, and with the twins about not recycling. He spent many months and lot of money custom-designing and supervising the installation of a recycling system throughout the house that makes it easier to recycle, easier to do the right thing. But still they don't seem to try or care as much as he thinks they should, and it frustrates him when he knows the future of the entire planet is at stake.

He recently started doing all the grocery shopping himself because he is more concerned about wasteful packaging than price. He saw apples in plastic tubes like tennis balls the other day, and it was so aggravating he found the store manager and complained. Truth be told, his encounter with the store manager was a bit loud and attracted the attention of other shoppers, but he didn't care. It was time he started being more vocal about these things, he decided. It felt strangely good.

His new project at work is the largest and most ambitious neighborhood development project in the history of the firm. He is responsible for building a whole new community, and he's determined to learn from and improve on his experiments at home. His goal is to create a model community known for setting a new standard for sustainable, green living.

All the expected things will be part of the plan of course. It's being built around a transit station, it will be walkable, and there will be a solar energy collection system that will actually produce more energy than the neighborhood needs. In theory, you would not need a car to live there, which may be a bit of a leap in this town where gas-guzzling SUVs are the university graduation gift of choice.

He wants to make it easier for everyone who will eventually live there to have a greener life without even thinking about it. He is convinced the answer is to incentivize the right behaviors and simultaneously complicate the wrong ones.

He lies awake at night thinking about how to do this.

ARCHETYPE OVERVIEW

Much has been written about environmental issues and the people who work tirelessly to save the planet. As a result, I think we all have a bit of a stereotype in our heads of what an environmentalist is like. The person in my head is a cross between Dr. David Suzuki, Meryl Streep, and the people who go to Burning Man every year.

But the 17 percent of the population who belong to The Environmental Assembly are far more nuanced. This is one problem inherent in writing a description for any archetype: trying to remove my own (or, when it's your turn, your own) preconceived notions.

Valuegraphics shows that environmentalists are focused on how the environment affects their family and vice versa. They are also very motivated by improving their own personal health and well-being, which I found to be a bit of a surprise, and I'm not sure why. Perhaps they feel a connection between the health and well-being of the planet and their own personal health and well-being, which, although rather meta, is a perfectly valid point of view.

A rare core value, one that we don't see very often, popped up here: a strong sense of personal responsibility. They feel that the environment is the most pressing issue of the day and that they personally need to do something about it.

Correspondingly, they think politics is a waste of time, and they don't bother to vote because they don't think that electing one politician over another will make a difference.

They are, however, highly educated and believe in the power of education. They want to know more, and they want to be more educated about how they can help the environment on a personal level. It must be overwhelming at times to care about something so deeply and not have the information they need to be able to impact the situation as much as they would like to.

They like gardening, maybe because it feels like one small way to reduce their carbon footprint. They tend to come from families with money, and they have little if any debt.

Curiously, they are very connected to whatever minority group they belong to. They may have taken an African name, learned to play the bagpipes, or joined a gay rights advocacy group. They volunteer within the groups they feel an affiliation with, maybe to find others there who are also committed to causes. While everyone they meet might not share their level of concern for the environment, at least they share a concern for something larger than themselves. And that's always a comfort.

CORE VALUES

1. Family
2. Health/Well-Being
3. Positive Environments
4. Personal Responsibility

CERTAINTIES

→ They are unlikely to support any major political party.

→ They place high priority on recycling and living cleanly.

→ They believe climate change is caused by humans, individually.

→ They are concerned about reducing their own carbon footprint.

LIKELIHOODS

→ They carry very little debt.

→ They are prone to grow at least some of their own food.

→ They are more likely to come from families with money.

→ They are highly educated but think there are flaws in the education system.

→ They strongly identify with any minority group to which they belong.

→ They don't bother with social media.
→ They consider themselves to be spiritual (but not religious).

IN THEIR OWN WORDS: REAL QUOTES FROM REAL SURVEY RESPONDENTS

→ "I was taught by my parents to respect everyone and every living thing. These are values I have passed on to my kids."
→ "If I stay healthy, I can be more productive and be a better person."
→ "The current state of the environment scared me into being more aware of the effect of my decisions."
→ "We all need to take responsibility for the results of our actions and do everything we can to limit the impact on those around us, and the earth."
→ "Stronger families make stronger communities."

HALL OF FAME

→ Al Gore
→ David Suzuki
→ Greenpeace
→ Elon Musk
→ Seventh Generation
→ Organic farmers everywhere

THE TECHNOLOGY FELLOWSHIP

→ 11% of the population

→ Agree on values 81% of the time

MEET LEEZA

Leeza gets concerned about things. It's sort of her jam. Everyone at the digital design agency where she works Monday to Friday thinks she's a bit of a loner, but it couldn't be further from the truth.

Every chance she gets, she's in one of the private chat rooms that she created to incite people in her community to organize around one thing or another. It usually has to do with preserving a historic building in her neighborhood or lobbying city officials to allocate more money to the playground down the street. At least that's what it's been about lately.

If all the historic buildings are torn down, she's worried it will change the way her community feels, and she likes the vibe on the streets around her apartment exactly the way it is. And that playground on the corner? It's become a magnet for all kinds of sketchy stuff. It needs better lighting and maybe even security cameras. She has no issues with security cameras if they are used for the betterment of society.

Where Leeza works is not really what Leeza considers to be her work. She even refers to it with her friends as her "income stream." As far as Leeza is concerned, her real work is doing what she can to rally her peeps and make the world a better place, locally or otherwise.

Sometimes her online gang of rabble-rousers, who number in the hundreds now, will flame someone on a social media channel who they think is threatening something they care about. She feels a rush of adrenaline when that happens. It feels good to be dishing out digital vigilante justice when it's deserved.

She remembers how powerful and involved she felt when she was one of the online organizers of Occupy Indianapolis. They didn't manage to attract the same national media attention that Occupy New York or some other cities did. But feeling part of a global movement to challenge the status quo? That made her jump out of bed early every morning, and stay up far later than she should have, with the glow from her laptop screen lighting her otherwise dark apartment.

ARCHETYPE OVERVIEW

I am old enough to remember when technology (as we think of it today) was a tiny little blip on the radar screen of the average person. There wasn't much of it around at all. My neighbor, Mr. Burgess, had a digital watch that my brother and I would ask him to show us whenever we saw him standing on the lawn in front of his house. A button on the side would make red digital numbers show up like magic from inside a ruby-black screen. It was the first time I had seen a watch with no hands.

The kids one year behind me in high school were learning how to use rudimentary computers, which seemed exotic and new. My classmates and I were much more mainstream, learning to type on what seemed like the most modern electric typewriters imaginable.

Today, anyone who isn't tethered to several devices and using digital tools all day long seems to be a bit of a throwback, or an intentional outlier trying to make a point.

The members of The Technology Fellowship are a unique breed of technology fans. They love their tech toys, but they don't love technology per se. They love and crave connections to others, and technology is a means to that end. Simply put, their relationships are largely via digital means. One data point that reinforces this insight is the importance of technology in their profile, despite the fact that they are not early adopters of technology. They are not in it for the tech; they are in it for the connections.

So of course, they rank belonging, community, and family highly. Other Valuegraphics Archetypes do as well, although not all in this particular order. For this group, family ranks third on the list, for example.

Interestingly, these values, which are all about membership in a group, extend to their political views. They lean toward socialism and "all for one, one for all" as opposed to the more singular democratic ideals of "one voice, one vote."

Technology isn't about media or entertainment for this group. It is purely and simply about connecting. Multi-player games, social media, Skype, and chat rooms about topics of interest, those all rank highly. They love being digitally connected to other people and will even be the social organizers if they feel this fellowship is lacking.

Once they have identified and bonded with others who agree with them about whatever their topic or issue might be, they are quite vocal about anyone who isn't on the same page. Star Trek Voyager fanatics will not take kindly to Star Trek Next Generation enthusiasts trying to dominate a conversation about Starfleet protocols.

CORE VALUES

1. Belonging
2. Community
3. Family

CERTAINTIES

→ They are primarily drawn to technology because it fosters relationships.

→ They have a strong altruistic streak and enjoy helping others.

→ They are not drawn to media technologies (e.g., Netflix).

→ They are not using technology for personal growth or entertainment.

→ They are unlikely to be voters.

LIKELIHOODS

→ They are big social media users.

→ They aren't likely to be early adopters of any technology unless it can clearly be shown to improve their relationships.

→ They often don't believe in democracy, preferring socialist ideas.

→ They like to band together, and they want to know who's in their tribe.

→ They are quick to make assumptions about people who are not in their tribe.

→ They are frequently the one in their group who plans events.

IN THEIR OWN WORDS: REAL QUOTES FROM REAL SURVEY RESPONDENTS

→ "My family introduced me to the concept that we are all part of something bigger, and we need to be responsible for that."

→ "Being a member of a tight community makes me feel secure."

→ "I look at my friends who are trying to achieve success in a corporate setting and see how stressed they are. I am more relaxed because I don't chase the same things."

→ "I believe we have a responsibility to future generations and that it starts with your local community."

→ "I am still trying to figure out who I am."

→ "Society is falling apart, and there is a lot of fear."

HALL OF FAME

→ Skype

→ Lady Gaga

→ Facebook

→ Anonymous

→ Mark Zuckerberg

→ Slack

→ Reddit

THE LEAGUE OF WORKAHOLICS

→ 10% of the population
→ Agree on values 80% of the time

MEET LOGAN

There's an old saying that Logan can't quite remember, but it has something to do with how you can only have two of the following: an amazing career, an amazing home, or an amazing relationship. Logan knows where he stands on that issue, and so does everyone who has ever met him.

His rise to fame and fortune came early in life. Almost shockingly so. He still runs into people from his graduating class at university who are jealous of how far he's gone and how fast. What they don't seem to understand is how he works "bloody hard and makes so many sacrifices" and has always done so. While they are off vacationing with the family at Christmas, he's quite happy to skip all that. He'd rather spend his time working and let everyone else grow fat on eggnog.

Logan's home is a trophy filled with trophies. He loves the adulation he receives whenever anyone comes to visit. Normally, the only people who see where he lives are associates or clients he is trying to impress. He specifically invites particular guests, so he can use his home as a kind of weapon to establish the alpha role for himself, an upper hand that might be advantageous.

Everything about his place is perfect. Everything is on brand. Everything important is purposefully placed to provide clear sight lines from all the vantage points where someone might stand, a Baccarat crystal martini glass in one hand and a crisply starched white linen Frette cocktail napkin in the other.

ARCHETYPE OVERVIEW

Before you jump to conclusions about The Workaholics, you should know that these folks tell us they wouldn't have life any other way. They love working long hours, love bragging about it, and they especially love buying the status symbols that show everyone how successful they are. They might be holdovers from the 1980s greed-is-good philosophical school, but they could just as easily be a new breed of entrepreneur that has defined work on their own terms and love every minute of it. I know people who are anxious when they aren't working because work is their drug of choice.

Don't get me wrong, these aren't misunderstood angels. Regardless of the varietal of workaholic we are talking about, they like the same things: money, toys, upward mobility, and visible signs of success. They will do anything they need to do to make sure they never sit in economy class on a commercial flight ever again.

They do not have a single core value that has anything to do with anyone else: no belonging or family or relationships. These are lone wolves who are looking out for number one. If they have tried their hand at marriage, it didn't work out. A marriage means caring about someone else, and this group doesn't do that.

It's not a big surprise to learn they aren't loyal to their employer and will move around to other firms at the drop of a (designer-made, expensive, fur-lined) hat.

If there are cracks in their self-reliant veneer, it's their desire to be thought of highly, or their delight in receiving awards. Yes, these traits could simply be seen as even more evidence of an egomaniacal personality. But it's also possible this enormous desire for recognition and respect stems from a deep-rooted fear, a fear that they aren't really as good as everyone thinks. Or really even good enough.

CORE VALUES

1. Financial Success
2. Material Possessions
3. Personal Growth
4. Upward Mobility

CERTAINTIES

→ They are extremely likely to work over eighty hours a week.

→ They are very likely to be single and possibly have been previously married.

→ They are not attracted to belonging.

LIKELIHOODS

→ About 50 percent of this group inherited their attitudes toward work from their parents.

→ They don't have much loyalty to their employer unless they're in the family business.

→ They cherish their accomplishments; about a third of them even recall their high school awards.

→ They may not care about belonging, but they do care about how they are perceived by others.

→ They tend to be highly educated.

→ They are not altruistic.

IN THEIR OWN WORDS: REAL QUOTES FROM REAL SURVEY RESPONDENTS

→ "I had early success in my career, and it motivated me to keep striving for excellence."

→ "Money opens doors, and miracles hide behind those doors."

→ "I like nice things, so I work hard to get them."

→ "People have high expectations of me, and that makes me work hard to meet those expectations."

→ "To achieve in this world, you need to continue to adapt and grow like I do. Keep up or go home."

→ "Money talks and I like to be loud."

HALL OF FAME

→ Jordan Belfort

→ Michael Jordan

→ Rolex

→ Berluti

→ Marissa Mayer

→ Rolls-Royce

→ American Express Centurion Card

→ Gordon Gekko

→ Martha Stewart

THE SAVERS SOCIETY

→ 13% of the population
→ Agree on values 76% of the time

MEET CLARISSA

Clarissa and her husband do their grocery shopping together on Fridays after Frank drives home from work. In addition to the groceries they need for the week, and any sale items they stockpile to avoid paying full price for the same things in the weeks ahead, they always buy two fancy donuts.

They have a ritual on Saturday mornings when the newspaper arrives. They like to sit together at the kitchen table and read the sections of the paper they each like best while enjoying their coffee and a donut.

Frank swallows his donut in two big bites. Clarissa

likes to pick at hers. She gets a bit of a thrill by not eating it all at once, a delicious pang of self-righteousness squeezed from the discipline of self-restraint. She wraps her donut in cling wrap on a saucer, places it in the refrigerator, and looks at it several times over the weekend until she decides she's ready to eat it. Sometimes she leaves it so long it's gone stale, and she throws it out, which makes her feel guilty. It's such a waste.

When Clarissa buys something at the mall, the first thing she does is call someone, usually her daughter, to tell her how much she saved. The amount she saves gives her a rush of dopamine, and it feels great, so she tells as many people as will listen. It feels like she's doing something illicit when she doesn't pay full price. "Guess what? I saved twenty-five dollars on a shirt! And it's lovely!"

When a friend or a member of her family gives her a flower arrangement, she hangs it upside down to dry as soon as it starts to wilt. That way she can enjoy the dried bouquets in vases all over the house for as long as she likes. They symbolize important occasions in her life, and she doesn't like it at all when someone suggests that at least some of them could be discarded.

She collects figurines of elephants too. Something about elephants calms her. She likes how they stare at her wisely from every shelf and sill in her home.

Elephants never forget.

ARCHETYPE OVERVIEW

Family, belonging, and financial security are the hallmarks of this target audience. They will avoid debt at all costs, sometimes going to extreme measures to save seemingly small amounts of money because "it's the principle." They will save up and wait for special sales before buying the things they want.

Be careful not to let the name of this group mislead you or limit your understanding. Yes, they do like to save money, but these folks savor saving. It's not a necessity but more a way of life.

They will be collectors. They will have a lot of friends and a big social network. They will save memories. Animals in distress. Empty margarine tubs and teacups with broken handles. Once someone or something comes into their life, it rarely leaves.

They are not attracted to the latest trends and technologies. Until the functional utility of some new technology is so great it can overcome the emotional satisfaction of having money in the bank, it's simply not something they are interested in. Unless, of course, it helps with saving.

For example, they were probably excited about the invention of smartphones with cameras and video-recording capabilities because it meant they could save more memories more often. And they would not hesitate to spend hard-saved dollars on a membership in a shopping club that promised discounts many times over whatever it cost to join.

Remember those three-inch-thick Treasure Chest coupon books for local restaurants, bars, and stores that schoolchildren flogged door to door to raise money for band camp? They always bought at least one and maybe a second one as a gift.

Part of their drive to save is because they always have one eye on the future. They are more likely than other groups to have come from non-European backgrounds and perhaps have lived through difficult times which they do not want to repeat. They are focused on retirement, despite the fact that retirement is becoming a rapidly archaic concept in contemporary life.

As an example of the sometimes oddball things we discovered throughout our research, we learned that these people inexplicably like wine more than any of our other archetypes. I don't have an explanation for that. Your guess is as good as mine.

CORE VALUES

1. Family
2. Belonging
3. Financial Security

CERTAINTIES

→ They are *not* attracted to the latest trends and technologies.

→ They share some characteristics with The Anti-Materialists Guild but are more attracted to possessions.

→ They do like possessions but generally not enough to use debt to purchase the things they want.

→ They can usually be found in a committed relationship, and they probably have kids.

LIKELIHOODS

→ They have at least one eye focused on retirement.

→ They usually won't make any major decision without first thinking about the future.

→ They generally save for security, not to purchase a particular item.

→ They expect their children to pay for their own college education.

→ They are likely to belong to a church congregation.

→ They often have a non-European heritage.

→ They enjoy drinking wine.

IN THEIR OWN WORDS: REAL QUOTES FROM REAL SURVEY RESPONDENTS

→ "I became a dad in my teens, and I learned the hard way that my decisions were about more than me. My kids always come first now."

→ "I want my kids to understand the value of every dollar and to be grateful for everything."

→ "For me, this is about knowing who you are and where you fit in the world."
→ "I don't know what comes next and that's the point."
→ "My husband works way too hard, and that worries me."
→ "I fight every threat to my family. Everyone should."

HALL OF FAME

→ Ebenezer Scrooge
→ Warren Buffett
→ Kia
→ Suze Orman
→ Winners
→ Benjamin Franklin
→ Walmart
→ Mr. Burns
→ Value Village

THE ROYAL ORDER OF THE OVERDRAWN

→ 14% of the population
→ Agree on values 76% of the time

MEET BRENT

Brent graduated from university full of vim. He was ready to take on the world, but he wasn't quite sure where or how yet. But success would come to him eventually, of that he was convinced.

He had a great time in university, swaggering through the requirements for his bachelor's of commerce degree. He made a lot of friends in class, on the basketball team, and on the weekends playing guitar in a folk rock band called Pork Belly Futures that he started with three of his business school buddies. Mostly, the band would smoke a lot of weed and crank out cover tunes in frat house basements, but it was fun to dive into this pseudo-rebellious side of his personality now and again.

His dad helped him land his first job as an intern on Wall Street working for a hedge fund. Those guys he worked for were rolling in cash while he was struggling to make ends meet. He felt obliged to take his turn buying drinks after work, but he was always broke. He had student loan payments and wasn't making millions. Still, he felt like he had to be one of the boys, and he considered those rounds of twenty-two-dollar martinis to be an investment in his future.

Brent's credit cards kept filling up, over and over, again and again. It wasn't only because of the drinks. Other things kept coming up.

For instance, he was invited to the senior partner's weekend home in Nantucket, and it would have been insane to say no to that. The other interns were not even invited, and it would be an amazing thirty-six hours of one-on-one time with all the guys who ran the company. But it wasn't exactly a free weekend. He had to buy gas for the car, bring an appropriately expensive gift, and he had to buy the right clothes for the occasion.

He skipped meals and did what he could to save money in ways that no one would notice. And he waited. It was only a matter of time until his big opportunity came along, and he'd be able to start living the dream.

Meanwhile, what could one more credit card hurt?

ARCHETYPE OVERVIEW

First, let me tell you how pleased I am with myself for the name I gave this archetype. It's my favorite name of them all. Basically, this group is drowning in debt, but I decided they deserved a little dignity, so I made them royal.

They value most highly their ability to meet their basic needs: food, clothing, and shelter. Although be aware that what people consider to be a basic need can vary wildly. BMW payments, a new smartphone, stylish clothes, vacations, and gym memberships are basic needs if you think they are basic needs. For others, enough to eat and money for the electric bill are all they are hoping for.

They would all love to be financially secure, but it doesn't ever seem to be within their reach.

It's also important to note that there are millionaires in this group as well as dishwashers working for minimum wage. Spending more than you earn has little relation to income.

Despite the sometimes-massive debt these people have accumulated, they still buy things they think they deserve and end up accumulating more debt as a result. They crave visible symbols of success.

A disproportionately high number of these folks are attracted to music, and while I can't explain why, the data indicates they very likely play a musical instrument. They are also keen on sports and enjoy participating in a good game as much as watching one.

Another outlying fact from our research: they are more

likely than average to enjoy recreational drugs and are proponents of legalization. Maybe recreational drugs offer temporary relief from worrying about debt? Or about anything else, for that matter.

CORE VALUES

1. The Ability to Meet Basic Needs
2. Financial Security (hopelessly)

CERTAINTIES

→ They have debts totaling at least double their annual income.

→ They are very attracted to material possessions.

→ They are NOT attracted to financial services.

→ They have accumulated debt that probably doesn't include student loans.

LIKELIHOODS

→ They typically are not highly educated.

→ They value friendships as highly as family.

→ They are uninterested in politics.

→ They are attracted to both playing and watching music and sports.

→ They are also attracted to drugs and are proponents of legalization.

→ They are big fans of video games, particularly of the interactive variety.

IN THEIR OWN WORDS: REAL QUOTES FROM REAL SURVEY RESPONDENTS

→ "Owning a lot of things means I am successful, and others will see that."
→ "I'm tired of things being tight. I don't want to be Bill Gates, but thinking beyond a tight budget for food and clothes would be nice."
→ "I want a new car!"
→ "I want my kids to have everything they want. Life is hard enough without them being disappointed on top of that."
→ "I long for the day when I can buy something nice and not put it on my Visa."
→ "We struggle to meet basic needs. What happens? We struggle, but we make it as a family because we have love, and we support each other."

HALL OF FAME

→ Speedy Cash
→ Visa
→ Pawn Superstore
→ Interns everywhere

Oddly, I can't think of a well-known person for the hall of fame, either real or fictional, because this archetype will disguise the state of their finances so well. Can you?

THE MORE THINGS CHANGE THE MORE OUR VALUES MATTER

VALUEGRAPHICS INDUSTRY PROFILES

In the previous ten chapters, I've outlined the top ten Valuegraphics Archetypes, the ten most aligned profiles that appear in the Valuegraphics Database. If you follow the DIY instructions and use the Archetype Ranking Tool included as Appendix 1, they will help your organization focus on some of the values that motivate your audiences to do the things they do.

But while those ten Valuegraphics Archetypes are useful tools, they are static, and the Valuegraphics Database is capable of so much more.

With all that data at our disposal, we can slice and dice datasets to answer all kinds of fascinating questions about what drives very specific target audiences to do the things they do, and how we can use that information to influence their decisions.

You see, human beings are very complex. Most people and most products, services, and brands fit into more than one archetype. Plus, there are all those other variables in the Valuegraphics Database that didn't make the top ten but might be of vital importance to a specific situation. Those two factors combined lead to an infinite number of specific profiles that can be developed.

For example, if we query just one layer deeper than the Valuegraphics Archetypes, we can learn what shared values drive the daily decisions of consumers in a particular industry.

THE VALUEGRAPHICS
OF NEW LUXURY

When I started writing this chapter, I looked at several sources for information on emerging trends in the luxury sector. Most of them pointed to a tectonic shift away from the commodification of luxury and toward something not yet fully defined. To help differentiate the before-and-after of this change, the industry has settled on the term New Luxury. That label, to my mind at least, means that anything from before must be Old Luxury.

Let's run with that.

Here's an illustrative example of a specific product within both the New Luxury and Old Luxury ecosystems: purses.

Fewer and fewer luxury consumers want the latest "it bag" anymore. That's an Old Luxury symbol of excess defined by the fact that everyone will recognize it, including those who can't afford to buy one themselves, which was more or less the whole point. It was about badging, and letting people know you belonged to a tribe that was at least partially defined by money.

Some sources within the New Luxury industry write about how it is embarrassing today to carry one of these recognizably expensive bags. One commentator, a blogger who writes about luxury goods with reverence, suggested these bags "scream for attention" and make the people carrying them look like they are "lacking in confidence."

I'm imagining a heat map of Manhattan that shows these shameful stockpiles of embarrassing Old Luxury handbags: huge hidden heaps of Birkin bags, Vuitton carryalls, and quilted Chanel bags shoved in the back corners of closets throughout the Upper East Side.

So what's the New Luxury equivalent? The New Luxury bag is a one-off (or at least hyper-limited-edition) purse, crafted by a charming yet salty, white-haired artisan with reading glasses on a chain over her white lab coat. She works in a tiny atelier in Paris. She's been making these bags—each one takes three months—since she was a girl, and she's nearly blind now. Her hands shake from stitching leather every day for sixty-five years.

There are no logos on the New Luxury bag, except a discrete tag inside that only the owner of the bag will ever see. Why? Because the rules of New Luxury dictate that the only people who should know your handbag cost as much as a new car for your nanny are the other four people who own the same one. And with any luck, they live in another part of the world so you never have to suffer the embarrassment of being at the same luncheon together.

Put another way, proponents of the idea of New Luxury talk about how luxury is no longer about badging yourself with conspicuous labels for the benefit of others. It is all about quality and craftsmanship and the best materials available, of course, but most importantly, it's now *all about you.*

The Valuegraphics Database backs up this anecdotal evidence, but with statistical values-based accuracy that brings facts into the conversation instead of opinions and guesswork. Our data analysis confirms that luxury consumers are looking inward and are more concerned with how an object or service makes them feel. New Luxury is about a personal experience with the product, service, or brand.

Specifically, the Valuegraphics Database points out that New Luxury is all about delivering three things:

→ Personalization
→ Customization
→ Uniqueness

Importantly, New Luxury is also more attainable for more people. New Luxury products, services, and brands don't necessarily come with price tags exclusively for the One Percent. As New Luxury replaces Old Luxury, democratization is coming along for the ride.

The database revealed that 25 percent of the total population of Canada and the USA are attracted to the idea of New Luxury to some degree. With a total binational population of roughly 360 million, that means there are ninety million people in the Total Available Market who are, or could be, New Luxury consumers.

Inversely, that means 75 percent of the people out there think that luxury by any definition is a bunch of hooey. They couldn't care less about any of this. So let's just take a deeper look at the ones who do. In an industry hungry for hard facts and data, maybe this information can help.

Under the personalization/customization and uniqueness umbrella, we found three New Luxury profiles that coalesced primarily around varying types of consumption: experiences, practical products, and non-practical products.

We've given them snappy names to make them easier to remember and talk about, and we've only included a couple of quick distinguishing characteristics from the full Valuegraphics Profile for each because the totality of what we learned could be a book unto itself. And perhaps one day will be.

THE EXPERIENCERS

There are a lot of experience junkies out there in many

industries today. We keep running into this characteristic in our work, profiling target markets for clients in a broad range of sectors.

The New Luxury Experiencers represent 7 percent of the overall population of Canada and the USA, or 27 percent of those who find New Luxury attractive. We are rounding things off here to keep the math simple, but either way you look at it, this group is roughly twenty-five million strong.

The Experiencers are like Goldilocks. They spend a lot of time and effort searching for experiences that are just right. The thrill of the hunt is as much a part of the experience as the experience itself.

The Experiencers want to talk about their experiential memories with others. In some ways, this takes the place of what the status handbag used to provide. It's an ego boost and an affirmation that they are indeed fabulously special. They subconsciously want other people to wish they could be more like them.

However, The Experiencers tell us they are quite concerned about showing off too much. They want to talk about their experiences just enough to get the verbal and emotional feedback they desire but no more. They don't want to overdo it and become known as that annoying party guest who is always trying to impress. But they do want to impress just enough to be admired. They are walking a very fine line.

Want to sell to the New Luxury Experiencers? Help

them feel like victorious hunters and design the customer experience so people will know all about it without your customers having to ever say a word.

THE PRACTICALS

The New Luxury Practicals represent 10 percent of the overall population of Canada and the USA, or 39 percent of those who find New Luxury attractive. Across Canada and the USA, this group represents roughly thirty-six million shoppers.

The Practicals will buy luxury brands without hesitation if they are convinced the product or service in question fills a practical need. This idea of practical luxury is an oxymoron to many, but in fact, it is quite historically aligned with the very beginnings of what we call luxury today.

While they may not have known it, our entrepreneurial ancestors who found a way to make better weapons were leveraging the shared values of The Practicals. Instead of relying on more easily available materials like copper, which is all bendy when used as a spearhead, or obsidian, which can cut things quite nicely but gets dull rather fast, they figured out a recipe to add a few different metals together under certain rules of mixology and make something superior, called bronze. This new, commingled material had immense practical value for weapons and tools. And it was, I would argue, one of the first luxury products, no doubt commanding a far greater number of goats in fair exchange than any practical implements that had come before.

Back to the present day, it is important to note that not only do The Practicals seek out luxury products and services that fit their Valuegraphics desires, but they also share an inverse and quite pronounced disinterest for material possessions of any sort. Unless, of course, those possessions have practical value. They could, in some circles, even be thought of as a rarefied type of Anti-Materialist, although that term does need to be taken in context.

Want to sell to the New Luxury Practicals? Avoid any suggestion that your product or service is luxurious and focus instead on why it is the best designed and best made tool for the job. The right practical object made perfectly for a well-defined purpose is worth paying top dollar for. Practicality and perfection-of-function is the only signifier the people who fit this profile are concerned with. Even the right pencil, if it does a better job of being a pencil than a normal pencil, will be highly coveted and respected by members of this Valuegraphics audience.

THE MATERIALISTS

Given our reading about the Old Luxury industry, we thought (incorrectly) that the New Luxury Materialists would make an appearance as a small handful of the population wrapped in Pucci shawls, shuffling along in Gucci loafers and clutching a Birkin under one arm as they slowly but regally made their way down the street.

But it turns out The Materialists are a whopping 9 percent of the overall population, or 35 percent of the total population of those who identified themselves as New Luxury prospects. So that means there are roughly thirty-one million, give or take a half-million, across Canada and the USA.

But something didn't seem quite right. How could it be that The Materialists were still such a significant part of the market when we see a never-ending stream of reports from the luxury industry pointing to their decline?

I found the answer in New York City.

I was staying at the New York Athletic Club, locked up in a guest room writing the book you are now holding in your hands. When hungry, I would leave my paper-strewn nest and zip across the street to the twenty-four-hour bodega to buy premade food scooped into plastic containers that were weighed at the cashier. Glamorous it was not.

This wasn't some fancy new age hipster reinvention of a bodega. It was more like the convenience store managed by Apu on the Simpsons, complete with fluorescent tube lights that buzzed overhead and a lone wiener rotating on steel rods under warming lamps. It was that kind of place.

But the people who worked there were friendly. They smiled at me when I walked in, looked me square in the eye, and said "thank you" when they handed me my change. Except for the haughty matriarch of the clan.

She had no time for me. No eye contact at all. She seemed to purposefully stare at the ceiling behind my head instead of acknowledging I was standing there at her cash register trying to pay for my containers of steamed broccolini, bottles of San Pellegrino, and bags of gummy bears. "Maybe it's because I'm a white guy?" I remember thinking to myself. "Or maybe it's because this is a neighborhood place, and I'm not from around here?"

But after the third or fourth visit, I saw the clue that let me decipher her attitude. It was right there in plain sight. Around her neck, hanging from a brilliant-cut serpentine chain, was a pendant the size of a twenty-five-cent coin, entirely covered in sparkly stones. In the center of this diamondesque display panel was the Chanel logo in bas-relief.

The bodega matriarch with the faux-Chanel necklace is a perfect example of Valuegraphics in action. That pendant wasn't made of real diamonds, but it sure made that woman into a princess. She is a New Luxury Materialist, and in ways that she can afford, she is using status-luxury symbols as a way to make herself feel important and successful. Her Chanel necklace reinforces her values and gives her what she needs.

We then found other studies that had proven a direct correlation between lower household income relative to one's neighbors and the purchase of high-status cars, riskier portfolios, and higher levels of debt. Another researcher found that in regions with higher levels of income inequality, more people searched Google for luxury brands.

In other words, the existence of such a large number of Materialists isn't only about the Queen of the Bodega. This is also about the stockbroker who has just graduated from university and leased a Porsche 911 Turbo instead of finding a more modest means of transportation, or the entrepreneur who is operating on credit but is trying to project success.

The Valuegraphics Database also revealed that The Materialists, like our Valuegraphics Archetype called The Savers Society, like to collect things.

However, they differ from The Savers Society around their collecting habits because they are only interested in collecting luxury objects that confer status. They are convinced these status objects are essential. In our Valuegraphics surveys, they highly rank status luxury products and services as a need, a want, and an expectation.

The Materialists use these status purchases to build and maintain a self-identity as collectors and connoisseurs of a certain product. It may feel like a rationalization to the rest of us, but you could argue that having the world's largest collection of Hermès handbags does make you a bit of an authority on Hermès handbags, which in turn earns you status points from others with similar aspirations.

They also told us they view luxury as a lifestyle, so much so that they will scrimp and save to get the status goods they desire. They wear their consumption as a badge of honor.

They additionally were very clear that they enjoy

talking about what they own, what they want to buy next, and what kind of service and recognition they expect from the brands they patronize.

Selling things to the New Luxury Materialists? I think the Old Luxury industry has this down cold. Keep up the good work.

THE VALUEGRAPHICS OF BRICK-AND-MORTAR BANKS

In pop culture, banks and bankers are often portrayed as the bad guys, so they don't generally elicit a lot of warm and fuzzy emotions. But you have to feel just a little bit bad for them given what's going on in their industry sector. They may still be making money, but like any of us, disruption is difficult, and the internet is muscling in on what used to be a pretty exclusive gig.

It all started in the early 1980s, when some progressive banks thought it might make things a bit more convenient for their customers if they offered some technological bells and whistles like cash machines. Before then, we had to stand in long lines during banking hours to get cash, which you had to do quite often, because everything was about cash. Credit cards weren't being handed out on street corners like they are today.

Fast-forward a few more years, and the banks decided this kooky internet thing was here to stay, and they started to add online services.

Initially, online banking services were quite rudimentary. You could move cash from one account to another and check your balance. Today, however, you can get approved for a mortgage or finance a small military coup from your smartphone while wearing your bathrobe and watching Oprah.

Online banking has become amazingly convenient. So much so that for the brick-and-mortar banks, what started out as a few digital extras has become a problem.

Unintentionally, by training us to love online banking features, we all started to see how bothersome brick-and-mortar bank branches were. They were never open at midnight when you needed more money for a last round of green apple martinis at the nightclub. And when they were open for what seemed like only a few terribly inconvenient hours every day, they were horrid. You had to fill out slips of paper with a pen attached to a bead chain and then stand in a lineup for your turn to talk through a barrier of steel bars to a teller who wielded official-looking rubber stamps and constantly had to scurry off and get a supervisor to initial something.

Ugh.

Today, you can use your fingerprint to access your account on your phone and deposit a check with your camera in about ten seconds. You can send money around the world to anyone by making up a password based on your favorite pizza toppings. You can chuck money into your retirement account or get your Visa limit increased in less time than it takes to wander into the kitchen and make a Nespresso.

Today, many successful banks don't have a brick-and-mortar presence at all and exist only as online entities. So why would anyone ever go to a brick-and-mortar bank ever again? It's a good question. And it's being asked with no small amount of fear and trepidation by traditional banks in their traditional bank boardrooms all across North America.

So I thought I'd see if I could use Valuegraphics to help sort this out.

We followed our standard methodology (see Appendix 3) and created a Valuegraphics Profile for people who still visit physical bank branches. Who are these people? What makes them tick? Can we convince more people to get back in the habit of actually visiting a bank?

What follows are just a few fun facts skimmed off the top of the deep audience profiles we created.

We found two distinct Valuegraphics Profiles for people who still visit bank branches in person. Let's call them The Wanters and The Needers.

While each Valuegraphics Profile is unique, they both

share one overarching similarity. Both audiences are motivated by *a desire for personal attention*. It is the *kind* of personal attention they are looking for, and the *rationale* for why they need that personal attention that creates the two separate Valuegraphics Profiles.

Let's pause here for a moment before we get into the profiles themselves.

If I was the CEO of MegaBankCorp and one of my objectives was to increase the number of people visiting bank branches in person, with even just the information in the previous paragraph, I'd immediately appoint a task force to figure out how to increase the personal attention customers receive when they walk through our doors. If more of our customers felt their values were being met, there would be far less chance of them switching to another bank.

Conversely, if I was the CEO of NewDigiBank.com, I'd have a team of engineers working around the clock trying to figure out how to make the online banking experience feel more personal and less digital. As convenient as online banking is, I never get to really like my bank or know the people who work there. I wonder if there's a digital workaround for that?

THE WANTERS

Here are just a few highlights from the Valuegraphics Profile for this audience.

The reasons why these people want to visit a bank

branch are varied, but what makes them into a defined profile is that regardless of why, they just want to bank this way. Two major sub-profiles appeared in the data: those who want to go to a bank because it's a social outing, and those who feel it is a more secure way to complete a bank transaction than the digital choices they may have.

Everyone in this profile highly values family, personal relationships, security, community, and happiness. Oddly, in all the Valuegraphics Profiles we create, happiness is a value that does not appear all that often. Despite that, the experience of banking makes these folks feel happy, or at least, that's what they would like.

If you are in the brick-and-mortar banking business, those are some pretty powerful cues for you already.

You see, in a Valuegraphics Profile, every word counts. When the data shows us that an audience highly values family, it means they *highly* value family. Not sort-of, or a bit, but *highly*.

How can you make visiting your bank branch into a family outing? Can you offer Saturday afternoon financial literacy classes for kids and involve crayons and cookies? Can you offer to link all the accounts of the members of a family who bank with your institution so that everyone gets a birthday bonus percentage point on savings balances when it's Aunt Edra's ninetieth birthday? Is there a reward for multigenerational family loyalty? Are you sending birthday cards to family members? Do you see where *just one* Valuegraphics data point can lead?

Back to the rest of the profile.

Simply because of a less frantic daily schedule, there are a disproportionate number of people in The Wanters who are older; however, the younger members of this group shared the same values overall. This seems like an opportunity that would be worth further exploration. It's not just about lonely old people. There are young people who are coming to the bank for the same sense of belonging, security, and happiness too.

When we dig around the data a bit more, it becomes apparent this group does not want to be rushed. They want tellers to remember their names, and they want to feel like a valued customer. As noted above, it's really less about the banking and more about the experience of banking. Just like with storefront retailers everywhere, a customer choosing to visit a bank in person is making an experiential choice. There's a lot of talk about the theatre of retail. What about the theatre of banking? Just like a shoe store, movie theatre, grocery store, office supply store, or gift shop, when I can get everything I need online, why would I ever set foot in a store again? MegaBankCorp needs to be asking themselves those same user-experience questions.

THE NEEDERS

This group of people is convinced they need to visit a bank branch in person, but they aren't entirely sure or united around the reason why. Not that it really matters why, because they perceive it to be a need, and that is what counts.

They share some of the same primary values with The Wanters: family, personal relationships, and financial security in particular, but they veer off and place a much higher value on material possessions and ambition.

Is it possible this group feels a need to visit a bank because it makes them feel successful and reminds them how ambitious they are? MegaBankCorp could find ways to leverage those emotional cues.

The Needers are very closely related to a Valuegraphics Archetype discussed earlier in this book, The Workaholics, one of the top ten profiles in North America today. The Workaholics are self-absorbed, want their success to be recognized, and they love status symbols. Perhaps the traditional aspects of banking in person are leveraging some of these values.

Could it be that going to the bank makes them feel successful simply because they like being seen in the bank? These days, after all, when banking doesn't need to happen in person, the idea that someone needs to go to the bank might be seen as (or be perceived as) an event or an occasion. A transaction that requires personal attention must be a very important transaction indeed.

This makes me think of Matt Damon.

In the Bourne movies, visiting the Swiss Bank was quite an occasion. There was a ritualistic nature to the initial greeting, replete with bowing, handshaking, and espresso-offering. The architecture and interiors were chosen to create a sense of security and grave seriousness. Footsteps echoed on marble floors. There were no potted geraniums, charity fundraising/drive posters with plush toys for prizes, or blue velvet cattle-herding ropes strung between stanchions.

The banks Bourne goes to are, instead, places of such severity they feel ceremonial. Secret code numbers are exchanged. Retina scans and fingerprint technologies confirm identities. Safety deposit box rooms are soundproofed, leather-lined, and situated behind a series of satisfyingly thick and heavy doors. The movie set designers relied heavily on a palette of gray, black, and steel.

Imagine if going to the bank made you feel like that.

I'm not part of this Valuegraphics Profile, but I'd make time to visit a bank that convinced me that, yes, my overdue electric bill payment is vitally important, and I am indeed as suave and international as Jason Bourne.

Unlike The Wanters, The Needers are not loyal to a particular branch or bank employee. They just want a bank experience that makes them feel that sense of importance they crave and meets their needs for speed and security. In other words, if you build it, they will come.

In a weird way, The Needers Valuegraphics Profile makes me think of people on airplanes who pull out their cell phone to call someone within a nanosecond of the wheels touching the ground to announce that they have landed. It makes them feel important.

Incidentally, I've noticed these tend to be the same people who rush off the plane as if on their way to perform emergency open-heart surgery, harrumphing if someone is walking too slow or impeding their progress, only to end up standing at the baggage carousel alongside everyone else, waiting for their suitcase to be regurgitated from the mysterious depths of the airport terminal.

THE VALUEGRAPHICS OF ARTS AND CULTURE

Full disclosure before we begin this section: the arts and culture sector is near and dear to my heart. I volunteer and donate as much as I am able within my community, I've raised funds for various groups, I even host events in my home to try and get more people addicted to various arts and cultural organizations. So if there is going to be authorial bias in any part of this book, it will be here.

A small bit of editorializing, because it's my book and I should get to do this at least once, and because I firmly believe that without the human values which arts and culture celebrate, we are lost.

These industries are meant to propel us forward,

make us think about ourselves and the world in ways we wouldn't otherwise spare a brain cell for, and open our minds to new and different ways of processing the human experience. But as if that weren't enough, this often-overlooked segment of the economy is vital to the financial health of our cities and towns. I've seen study after study that tracks each dollar invested in the arts, as it creates an enormous ROI for the municipality or region concerned.

It has been proven conclusively that kids do better in math and science if they are also studying music and art. Yet, we continue to reduce funding or entirely delete these programs in our schools.

Neurologists will tell you that a simple new experience, even as simple as walking to work on the other side of the street from the side you usually choose, is enough to trigger the formation of new neural pathways in your brain. Your brain changes, and you become something more. So just imagine the burst of neural pathway formations that must occur when you are faced with artworks or performances that are unlike anything you've seen before. The opportunity to find mysteries that are still unexplainable in our contemporary world should be embraced, and if these encounters with the unknowable make your brain bigger too, why wouldn't we want as much of this stuff as we can get?

Art, in all forms, is good for all of us, and it is an essential part of what it is to be human.

However, like many sectors of the economy, arts and culture industries are being disrupted. New forms of entertainment are popping up every few minutes, it seems, and it's so much easier to zone out and binge-watch a new alien-zombie-police-time-travel series on Netflix from the comfort of your sofa than it is to put on your pants and go see a play, or visit an art exhibition and be challenged.

Plus, we just aren't learning how to consume art forms anymore. The most common conversation I have when trying to win new converts to this sector is about the fear of "not getting it," or some kind of generalized confusion about how to watch, look, or listen to something new. There was a time when we all knew how to listen to a string quartet or look at a sculpture. But we are losing those skills.

Consequently, the sector is losing ground with younger generations who find it all a bit overwhelming and unfamiliar, and misguidedly, the rallying cry around the boardroom tables of the arts and culture sector seems to be "we need to engage the millennials."

Based on Valuegraphics data from 75,000 surveys, I respectfully disagree with these tactics. When the symphony or theatre company decides serving quinoa hotdogs and having a hip-hop DJ at intermission is the answer, because "that's what millennials like," I know it's well-meant. But millennials, as I've discussed throughout this book, are a myth. They don't all like the same things or even agree on what is important any more than 15 percent of the time. Targeting an age group with stereotypical ideas about what they like is clearly not going to provide the boost that the sector needs.

Instead, arts organizations should find ways to meet and exceed the values of the following Valuegraphics Profiles. This will work, and it has nothing, or at least microscopically little, to do with age.

There are three distinct Valuegraphics Profiles to review—The Purists, The Talkers, and The Experience Seekers. As with the previous profiles on luxury and banking, what I've included here is just a quick snapshot of what the full Valuegraphics Profiles for arts and culture audiences revealed, but I hope it helps.

This is not always the case, but the three profiles we uncovered in the Valuegraphics Database are quite straightforward and related directly to motivation. This makes it easier for arts administrators and boards to develop programs to target these audiences because the connection between the profile and a corresponding action is quite clear. No rocket surgery (my new favorite descriptor) is required here, just some fresh ideas about reinforcing the values for each profile.

THE PURISTS

The purists are an easy audience to understand, and they're also an easy audience to impact. They are the cognoscenti, the experts (self-proclaimed or otherwise) in an art form who will notice if some aspect of the experience is not the same as it once was or is not what they think it ought to be.

Most of us wouldn't be able to talk intelligently about the tempo of the third movement of a Mozart symphony or the decision to paint the walls for an art exhibition at the public gallery gray instead of the more usual dull white. But these folks will. They know how to consume the art form they love, they love the art form they know how to consume, and they are the most likely to stay true to the art form that holds the most special place in their heart.

I have a theory that their expertise around a particular art form is what gives them comfort. It feels good to be the smartest guy or girl in the room at intermission or at the opening reception. But that feeling of being in-the-know is what makes the opportunity to cross-pollinate this audience between art forms very tangible. It wouldn't take much to point out the similarities between, say, contemporary painting and contemporary dance, and thereby make it clear to this group that the knowledge they already have is more transferable than they might think. They can be the smartest person in more than one room with very little effort.

For this group, it's not about being seen, or sharing the experience with anyone, although they aren't openly opposed to either of those scenarios. They are there for the art itself, regardless of other factors that may or may not be present.

Of all the Valuegraphics Profiles we have worked on, sadly this is one where age does seem to matter to some degree. The Purists tend to be over the age of forty-five, which still means we will find them in multiple generations. But as a society, it raises a red flag that we are not being exposed to arts and culture from a young age anymore. We are not making new Purists.

We also know that The Purists are financially secure, extremely likely to be in a committed relationship, and are career professionals. They are somewhat materialistic and well-travelled.

So how can an arts organization go about keeping The Purists they already have? By filtering everything through the primary values of this audience profile: *family, relationships, and creativity*. The specific responses will depend on the organization and art form in question. Simply convening a group of interested parties to brainstorm specifically about how to offer more of those three values would undoubtedly yield actionable results.

How could an arts organization go about creating new Purists? Opportunities to learn how to consume an art form could be offered. I was lucky enough to have someone spend hours talking with me about how to watch contemporary dance and how to consume the art form. Another charismatic figure in my life explained to me late one night over a glass of red wine how to listen to the piano. And yet a third individual taught me, over many brown-bagged lunches, how to look at a painting. My life has been richer for those lessons ever since.

A glimpse behind the scenes is often a great way to make people feel more connected to the art form in question. Explanations and stories that put art into context would be a smart tactic to pursue, despite the most fanatical Purists who don't think things should be explained, just experienced. We all have to learn from somewhere, and insider knowledge is one of the easiest ways to create that sense of belonging we all crave, regardless of the product, service, or brand in question.

THE TALKERS

The Talkers are almost the exact opposite of The Purists. They are primarily motivated by, and place a high value on, the stories they can tell as a result of their consumption. They consume to say that they have consumed, and they will talk about it to whoever will listen. Arts organizations need to find ways to give them what they want: as many stories to tell other people as they can possibly cope with.

The Talkers have quite a different set of characteristics and values than The Purists, and bluntly, offer a more lucrative revenue generation opportunity for arts and culture organizations to pursue. Here's why.

This group will spend more on tickets to an event to get the best seats or some kind of VIP experience, which is always good for the bottom line. Even better, they are very active on social media because it is a great platform to tell a lot of people what they have done. In a way, they are paying for the opportunity to have something special to talk about, become spokespeople, and assist in your marketing efforts.

The key to the Talkers Valuegraphics Profile is, of course, their values. They are most motivated by *personal growth, relationships, and possessions.*

Three very broad ways to leverage the values of this profile would be to:

→ Create a memento of their premium-priced VIP experience for them to take away and show to others.
→ Give them opportunities to strengthen relationships and make new friends.
→ Find an element of learning or personal growth to inject into your experience design.

I think most arts organizations, at least the ones I am involved in or aware of, do a fairly good job of this. It's nice to know that the data from 75,000 surveys backs up how important this segment of the arts and culture audience is, and that the efforts being made to court them are in line with what the Valuegraphics data analysis revealed.

THE EXPERIENCE SEEKERS

We see Experience Seekers pop up frequently in the Valuegraphics Profiles we extrapolate from the database for various clients. They are prevalent in most industries and in most situations.

It's interesting to see them appear as a separate group here, however, as all arts and culture audiences of all kinds are in it for the experience in one way or another. To have a data spike around a group of experience seekers in a sector that is all about experiences must mean these are experience junkies of the most extreme kind.

They are similar to The Talkers profile, except that the motivation for the experience isn't to share what they've done with others. They are in it for themselves. They are intrinsically motivated, not using the experience as a form of extrinsic badging.

They share core values of *family, relationships, and community*. What appeals to this group the most is the uniqueness of the particular event or experience as it relates to their family, relationships, and community.

They will come and see the same play more than once if it features a version for date night with the spouse, and another with a slightly different experiential tone that works for a family outing too. They want to come to new art exhibitions they haven't seen before, in places they've never been before, using technologies they are unfamiliar with, especially if somehow this all leads to building a sense of community. They want a different experience than the last time, and they are looking for an experience that promises a fresh perspective, a unique setting, or an unheard-of twist on a classic.

CUSTOM VALUEGRAPHICS PROFILES

When commissioned to profile a precise target audience for a specific product, service, or brand, the Valuegraphics Database can reveal game-changing insights.

For ethical reasons, I can't include too much detail here. The profiles we have extrapolated for clients are proprietary, and, more often than not, the finer points of a Valuegraphics Profile for a particular product, service, or brand will only be of interest to the organization it was created for. But with a few clever disguises, and a change of names to protect the innocent, I have been able to cherry-pick a few details to share. Each one is just a single highlight from a much more complex report, but nevertheless, they illustrate the point: Valuegraphics can be used in an extremely customized way.

THE SWIMMING POOL THAT BECAME MORE THAN A SWIMMING POOL

Like all apartment buildings in this particular parched, desert metropolis, a specific real estate rental development had plans for a large and luxuriously furnished swimming pool on the roof deck.

Valuegraphics revealed that the target audience for these apartments highly valued their own creativity, and offering the potential to exercise that personal creativity was key to influencing their decisions about all things.

The design and messaging for the pool area avoided presenting the swimming pool as a palm-tree festooned place to relax on a chaise and mingle with friends and neighbors. Instead, this swimming pool was envisioned and described as a place to get out of your creative headspace, do something physical, and return to your current creative pursuit with a clear and refreshed mind. In fact, all the amenities and common areas were chosen, programmed, and described in a way that leveraged how they might make your creative life richer.

WHEN THE PATH OF LEAST RESISTANCE IS ALSO THE ROAD TO RICHES

For a subscription-based online retailer of decorative housewares, the Valuegraphics Database revealed a target audience comprised of two related profiles with one key distinction.

One audience profile saw themselves as collectors of this household item and enjoyed hunting for rare and unusual additions to their collection. The other audience profile saw this category of merchandise as something that simply needed replacing periodically, saw it as a bit of a chore, and valued the ease of the subscription home-delivery model.

Both groups highly valued the praise they would receive from friends and family for freshening up the look of their home on a regular basis. However, the collectors would need to feel very actively involved in sourcing, curation, and selection, while the replacers would just be passively happy that things matched and looked good.

In other words, one group would require far more customer service, interaction, and collaboration, and the other wouldn't. Guess which audience this company focused on for the design of their service model, branding, and messaging?

VALUEGRAPHICS IN AN INDUSTRY BUILT ON FLUCTUATING VALUES

For a multinational hedge fund, institutional investors who control the placement of enormous sums of money are the holy grail. They are notoriously hard to reach, and the fund industry, in general, relies on almost interchangeable documents called *pitch decks* to plead their case.

For the decision makers faced with dozens if not hundreds of pitch decks on their desk or in their inbox, it can be hard to tell one "amazing opportunity" from the next.

We uncovered three Valuegraphics Profiles comprised of senior-level institutional investors who have a hand in deciding where these vast sums of money go. Following are very condensed generalizations of the full report.

One audience values being able to project an image of success by acquiring status symbols, talking about the status symbols, and telling anyone who will listen about the next status symbol they hope to acquire. Why have a platinum credit card when a titanium credit card is so much more satisfying?

The second audience we uncovered values career advancement and stability. This is their dream job, and they will do whatever they must do to keep it. They want to move up the ladder to positions of even greater responsibility. They won't even mentor a younger generation for fear of grooming someone who may one day compete for their job.

The third audience places an extremely high value on what they perceive as the creative aspects of what they do. I had one workshop participant from this company who stood up and talked about how the complex mathematical formulas they work with every day are like poetry or music. Mathematics, he argued, was the ultimate and original art form.

Here was a member of the Valuegraphics Profile come to life, standing right in front of me in human form.

The conclusion for this hedge fund was to build a very exclusive brand that offered prestigious and serious invitation-only opportunities to improve the skillset of certain hand-selected institutional investors and to thematically connect mathematical complexity to other forms of artistic expression. Without getting into specifics, this satisfied the values of all three Valuegraphics Profiles—status, career advancement, and creativity.

WHY CAN'T WE ALL JUST GET ALONG?

A very large foreign brand had relocated to a cosmopolitan city where the influence of foreign investment was regarded with great fear and even active protests. Valuegraphics Profiles of the community pointed to the exact values the locals felt were under threat and crucially were also understood to be hallmarks of the national culture of the foreign company who felt under siege.

In other words, Valuegraphics data was able to prove which values were shared by the company and the community. The company was then able to build a brand based on those areas of alignment.

A TASTE OF MY OWN MEDICINE

After almost two years of working with the Valuegraphics Database, I had the brilliant idea of using Valuegraphics to figure out who would be interested in Valuegraphics. I feel like an idiot for not thinking about this sooner, but since we are such good friends now, I don't mind admitting that I was slow to come up with this idea.

We profiled just one potential group of Valuegraphics users: people who had attained at least the rank of Vice President of Marketing at a large corporation. What we found out was quite illuminating, and thankfully, everything more-or-less reinforced the decisions we had already made.

I was able to frame my messaging and public speaking around values that I *knew for a fact* would resonate with this audience, instead of just what I suspected would perk up their ears.

In brief, what we discovered was that this audience is most intrigued with Valuegraphics because it is an entirely new and innovative tool that has never been available before.

They are also very cautious, as well they should be with anything that breaks so dramatically with the status quo. They want proof that Valuegraphics provides customized information unique to their own specific target audience, not just more of the vague and generalized demographic profiling information they already had plenty of.

Of all the things they might want to know, we discovered that what they valued most was the risk mitigation that Valuegraphics brings to an entire business plan by more accurately predicting how a precisely defined target audience will react to specific initiatives. The guesswork is gone.

Our inquiry revealed three Valuegraphics Profiles for this particular prospect audience, and without boring you to tears, following is a quick synopsis.

The first audience has moved from place to place extensively for work and experienced many cultures, so they understand the danger of using empty stereotypes as a profiling tool better than most. They see Valuegraphics as wise and highly portable as they move on to their next job somewhere else.

The second audience values how innovative Valuegraphics is because they highly value the jet fuel it could add to their career advancement. They believe that introducing Valuegraphics to their organization could be the factor that catapults them to the next level on their career trajectory.

The third audience believes their job as a marketing leader is to connect with their target audiences on a very personal level. They see Valuegraphics simply as a very logical thing. They don't even really think of it as innovative. They see it more as a necessity.

I have met people from all three of these profiles before. As I encounter more of them in the future, I will know which messages will be the most motivating. It will make me look much smarter when I can talk specifically to the values they are most interested in hearing about.

FIVE WAYS VALUEGRAPHICS WILL HELP YOUR ORGANIZATION

1. **Valuegraphics will multiply your budget effectiveness.** For every dollar you spend targeting an audience, like baby boomers who only agree on anything 13 percent of the time, you can now reach an audience that agrees on everything as much as 89 percent of the time. That's like multiplying your budget seven or eight times over.

2. **Valuegraphics simply works better.** Use Valuegraphics to profile your target audience, and you'll motivate the people you want to reach with seven or eight times

more efficiency than you will if you rely on age as a profiling tool.

3. **Valuegraphics mitigates planning risk.** Many parts of the organizational planning process are based on gut feel or the opinion of the most powerful person in the room. Valuegraphics mitigates that risk by adding statistical proof to the equation. Evaluating how a target audience or stakeholder group will react to an initiative should not be based on "Leanne from accounting fits this demographic. What does she think?" or "The CEO wants it this way."

4. **Valuegraphics fuels innovation.** Now that we can more accurately predict reactions from a target audience, we make it less scary to try new and innovative ideas. A culture of innovation is a highly desirable thing during disruptive times like these.

5. **Valuegraphics can eliminate arguing and politics.** I've lost track of the number of times I've presented to a boardroom of executives who give me feedback, like "My wife hates that," or "It's great, but there's something not quite there yet." Those of us who deal in ideas for a living know how to counter with our own opinions, of course, but eventually, the client will win, as they are the ones wielding the checkbook. With Valuegraphics, ideas generated internally or externally can be based on data that supports their audience-motivating appeal. It saves time and money and reduces the strain on working relationships. All good things.

IT'S LATE AT NIGHT ON FRIDAY...

It's late at night on Friday at the marketing firm, and everyone on the project team has already left the office except for one writer.

An enormously important branding presentation is due next week, and after months of meetings, due diligence, and briefings, the lone writer is throwing pencils at the ceiling trying to find inspiration. All he really wants to do is ditch the office and go to his Ultimate Frisbee league finals in the park. After a few suitably Herculean attempts to bash out a clever and snappy headline, he's done all he can do with the information he's been given. He closes his laptop and hopes his work will be approved in the morning.

Valuegraphics isn't going to change how many multi-million-dollar decisions come down to the ideas of just one or two people who must process reams of information and do what they do best. But a Valuegraphics Profile briefs these big thinkers with more of the right kind of information about what the end user values, what motivates them the most. With Valuegraphics data, they will be equipped to trigger the desired audience reaction, because what we value determines what we do.

Valuegraphics offers the same laser focus on audience values to fuel the work of the architect, the interior designer, the landscape team, the product designer, the brand manager, the marketing vice president, the small business owner, the visionary CEO, or any other professional who deals in that most subjective and fickle of all currencies—ideas.

Use Valuegraphics to make every decision you possibly can for every aspect of your organization: HR, internal culture, marketing, branding, product development, R&D, everything. If you do, you will have a beautifully aligned, values-centric organization offering your audience a product or service they want, built on the values you share.

The more things change, the more our values, which don't change so easily, will become the only thing we can rely on. It's that simple. It always has been that simple. The only thing new is the Valuegraphics ecosystem of algorithmic data that allows us to do a more scientific job of it.

I hope Valuegraphics makes all your ideas, and our whole world, exponentially better.

DAVID ALLISON 2018

APPENDICES

APPENDIX 1

DIY VALUEGRAPHICS
ARCHETYPE RANKING TOOL

INSTRUCTIONS FOR USE

The DIY Valuegraphics Archetype Ranking Tool is a very simple survey you can use with an audience of customers or employees to determine which Valuegraphics Archetypes they resemble most.

Remember, this is just a way to rank order the Archetypes, and it is not meant to be a precise analysis of your audience's Valuegraphics Profile. It will not hold up to a statistician's expectations.

It's like an artist opening a drawer and discovering a lot of red paint, almost as much blue, a bunch of green, and then some yellow, purple, and silver, with almost no brown or pink to be seen. It does *not* tell you how the colors combine or what kind of painting these colors could become. But it's a start.

Collect as many completed surveys as you can. Then total the responses to see how the Archetypes rank. Tabulation instructions are in the answer key.

Start to think about your company based on the archetype rankings this tool produces. From hiring to marketing, from product design to customer service, Valuegraphics will help you become a more values-centric organization, and this is a first step in the right direction.

If you are interested in having a custom Valuegraphics Profile created especially for your target audience, we'd love to talk. Using our database of 75,000 surveys, we'd see how the colors in your paint box combine, in what quantities, and with what levels of intensity. We'd create a very specific portrait of the values of your audience and help you motivate more people more often.

THE DIY ARCHETYPE RANKING TOOL QUESTIONS

For each of the ten statements that follow, please circle a number from one to ten that represents how you see yourself in relation to that statement. There are no right or wrong answers. Your first reaction is correct!

Take your time and please choose only one number for each question.

I am curious, restless, and like to try new things, eat at new places, and meet new people. I like to belong to groups, and I'm not very political.

NOT LIKE ME AT ALL—1 2 3 4 5 6 7 8 9 10—VERY MUCH LIKE ME

I don't feel as much at home as I'd like, in all kinds of ways, and I'm not sure why. **I feel a bit unsure about the future.**

NOT LIKE ME AT ALL—1 2 3 4 5 6 7 8 9 10—VERY MUCH LIKE ME

I am not into having stuff, owning stuff, or collecting stuff. **Stuff weighs me down.** Besides, experiences are more important than things.

NOT LIKE ME AT ALL—1 2 3 4 5 6 7 8 9 10—VERY MUCH LIKE ME

I have had the same job for a long time. **I like things to stay the same.** I like my friends and pretty much all aspects of my life as they are.

NOT LIKE ME AT ALL—1 2 3 4 5 6 7 8 9 10—VERY MUCH LIKE ME

I am happiest when I have time to be creative. It's one of the most important things in my life. I hate being bored. I spend a lot of time thinking about things that intrigue me. It helps me grow as a person to express myself creatively.

NOT LIKE ME AT ALL—1 2 3 4 5 6 7 8 9 10—VERY MUCH LIKE ME

The environment is the issue of our time, and the only answer is for each of us to do our part. I wish I knew how I could help more. The politicians aren't going to take care of this for us. We all have to change how we live.

NOT LIKE ME AT ALL—1 2 3 4 5 6 7 8 9 10—VERY MUCH LIKE ME

I'll admit to having a lot of technology in my life. But I'm not really a technology person. **I stay connected with my friends and family** with social media and other channels because I feel out of the loop if I don't.

NOT LIKE ME AT ALL—1 2 3 4 5 6 7 8 9 10—VERY MUCH LIKE ME

I work a lot. But I don't mind, because it means I can live the life I choose. I like having nice things. **I'm one of those career-first people.**

NOT LIKE ME AT ALL—1 2 3 4 5 6 7 8 9 10—VERY MUCH LIKE ME

I try and save as much money as I can, even if it means a little bit of inconvenience. You never know if tomorrow is going to be a rainy day.

NOT LIKE ME AT ALL—1 2 3 4 5 6 7 8 9 10—VERY MUCH LIKE ME

I'd like to save money, but it seems impossible! There's always something coming up that can't be avoided. And besides, **what's the point if you can't splurge from time to time?**

NOT LIKE ME AT ALL—1 2 3 4 5 6 7 8 9 10—VERY MUCH LIKE ME

THE DIY ARCHETYPE RANKING TOOL ANSWER KEY

The order of the survey questions corresponds with the order of the Valuegraphics Archetypes below.

Here's how to tabulate the responses: if five people each circled 10, 5, 6, 1, and 2, then the total score for that question and corresponding Archetype is 24. Total the scores for each of the ten questions, and you'll see which archetypes are more dominant in your audience.

→ The Adventure Club

→ The Home Hunters Union

→ The Anti-Materialists Guild

→ The Loyalists Lodge

→ The House of Creativity

→ The Environmental Assembly

→ The Technology Fellowship

→ The League of Workaholics

→ The Savers Society

→ The Royal Order of the Overdrawn

APPENDIX 2

VALUEGRAPHICS DATABASE COMPOSITION

Nothing makes my eyes glaze over like a table filled with numbers, but there are people who enjoy all those columns and rows. So if you are like me, I apologize in advance for what comes next, and if you are a *table junkie*, this is your lucky day.

In the following pages, I've included a few tables to give you a sense of the wide diversity of the 75,000 people in the Valuegraphics Database. The most important thing to remember is this: the survey respondents were collected to mimic, or statistically represent, the populations of Canada and the USA.

That's important, because it means that every Valuegraphics Profile we extrapolate from the database will be true. Assembling this much data had been impossibly expensive and time-consuming until the advent of algorithmic technologies, but now that we've done it, all our findings will be accurate to **within +/- 3 percent and with a 95 percent degree of confidence.**

GENERATIONS	OVERALL	CANADA	US
Greatest Generation (1915–1927)	1%	1%	1%
Silent Generation (1928–1945)	5%	4%	5%
Boomers (1945–1964)	27%	28%	27%
Generation X (1961–1979)	28%	28%	26%
Millennials (1980–1995)	31%	33%	32%
Generation Z (1996–1998)	8%	6%	9%

Note: As we only survey those eighteen and older, Gen Z was limited to three years.

UNITED STATES		CANADA	
Northeast US	28%	Western Canada	40%
South US	22%	Central Canada	35%
Midwest US	18%	Atlantic Canada	17%
West US	32%	Northern Canada	6%

Note: Geographic quotas were applied to ensure we had a representative sample from all regions of Canada and the USA. In cases where we have enough surveys from a city, we can extract Valuegraphics data at the civic level too.

EMPLOYMENT STATUS	OVERALL	CANADA	US
Full-Time/Self-Employed	41%	42%	39%
Part-Time/Contract/Casual	15%	19%	10%
Student	14%	15%	13%
Retired	14%	11%	16%
Unemployed	12%	9%	14%
Full-Time Parent	6%	4%	8%

EMPLOYMENT INDUSTRY	OVERALL	CANADA	US
Accounting/Finance/Banking	3%	2%	4%
Architecture/Design	2%	1%	3%
Arts/Leisure/Entertainment	4%	3%	4%
Beauty/Fashion	4%	3%	4%
Construction	7%	9%	5%
Consulting	2%	2%	1%
Customer Service	6%	8%	4%
Distribution	3%	2%	3%
Education	10%	11%	8%
Healthcare	11%	9%	13%
Management (Senior/Corporate)	14%	15%	12%
Media/News/Information	2%	2%	1%
Operations/Logistics	4%	3%	5%
Other	2%	2%	2%
Planning (Meeting, Events, etc.)	2%	1%	2%
Production	5%	4%	5%
Real Estate	4%	3%	4%
Research	4%	3%	5%
Restaurant/Food Service	9%	10%	8%
Sales/Marketing	3%	4%	2%
Science/Technology/Programming	3%	2%	3%
Social Service	2%	1%	2%

GENDER	OVERALL	CANADA	US
Female	52%	51%	54%
Male	46%	48%	44%
Third Gender/Unspecified/Other	2%	1%	2%

ETHNICITY	OVERALL	CANADA	US
European	54%	54%	51%
Hispanic	10%	7%	14%
African-American	10%	7%	12%
Asian	9%	9%	8%
Native American/First Nation	8%	10%	5%
Middle Eastern/Arab American	5%	7%	3%
Hawaiian/Pacific Islander	3%	2%	3%
Other	3%	4%	4%

EDUCATION	OVERALL	CANADA	US
Doctorate or higher	1%	1%	1%
Masters or equivalent	3%	4%	3%
Bachelor's degree or equivalent	18%	21%	14%
Associate degree or equivalent	14%	9%	12%
Some college/university, no qualification	7%	8%	9%
Diploma or equivalent	3%	6%	4%
Certificate or equivalent	4%	3%	3%
High school qualification	11%	14%	15%
No qualification	39%	34%	39%

INCOME	OVERALL	CANADA	US
Less than $25,000	23%	22%	24%
$25,000 to $34,999	22%	19%	24%
$35,000 to $49,999	16%	15%	17%
$50,000 to $74,999	12%	10%	13%
$75,000 to $99,999	15%	21%	10%
$100,000 to $124,999	7%	8%	6%
$125,000 to $149,999	4%	3%	5%
$150,000 +	1%	2%	1%

APPENDIX 3

VALUEGRAPHICS DATABASE RESEARCH METHODOLOGY

The research we did for this book started with a hunch: that traditional age-based profiling of target audiences does not work as effectively as it once did. Nobody acts their age anymore, so why use age to predict how people will act?

If we could statistically prove that to be true, we thought, it would mean traditional audience profiling methods for products, services, and brands would need to be rethought.

Turns out our hunch was right. Analysis of the data proved that traditional profiling tools based on age or generational cohorts does not work in contemporary times.

Age is largely irrelevant as a determinant of behavior, and for the first time, we have proof.

Perhaps even more interesting, we also found that when we create target audience profiles based on shared values, the people in those groups agree with each other on nearly all their other wants, needs, and expectations too.

We had discovered a better way. We decided to call this new values-based profiling system Valuegraphics.

Elsewhere in this book, we've briefly explained how we created Valuegraphics by initially asking 40,000 people what they value, want, need, and expect from life.

What follows here is a more detailed description of our methodology, for those who are interested in the finer points of our process.

SURVEYS

A total of ten surveys were launched, beginning in June 2016. Each of these surveys had a specific theme, for example: finance, education, or recreation. We also did a couple of follow-up surveys to explore some of the findings more deeply, but those first ten surveys are what matter most.

QUESTIONS

Across these surveys, a total of 340 questions were asked about all aspects of what it means to be a human being alive today and what people value, want, need, and expect. The questions were derived from proven social-science tools: the World Values Survey, the World Happiness Index, the Bhutan Gross Domestic Happiness Index, and various other established studies.

Every valid respondent answered the values-based questions, and we used the resulting data to identify the ten Valuegraphics Archetypes who agree on a statistically impressive number of values, wants, needs, and expectations. In other words, we found ten huge groups of people who agree on pretty much everything.

We continuously access the data pool to create Valuegraphics Profiles that can help organizations understand how to more effectively motivate the people they want to impact. Each time we extract data, more insights are uncovered, and our understanding of how to motivate people improves. At the time of writing this section of the book, in April of 2018, the database now contains 75,000 surveys and continues to grow.

NUMBER OF RESPONDENTS

Over 35,000 surveys from the primary recruitment wave were deemed valid and complete. We added additional surveys on certain intriguing values, and a follow-up survey to better understand certain aspects of the data revealed by the initial analysis. All told, we ended up with responses from more than 40,000 surveys in our foundational data pool.

Since roughly 1,850 surveys would be a more-than-sufficient sample size to statistically model the population of Canada/USA, our data pool of 40,000 should be considered exhaustive.

GENERATIONS OF RESPONDENTS

In order to ascertain if age impacted responses to other questions, each respondent was asked for their year of birth.

GENERATIONS	OVERALL	CANADA	US
Greatest Generation (1915-1927)	1%	1%	1%
Silent Generation (1928-1945)	5%	4%	5%
Boomers (1945-1964)	27%	28%	27%
Generation X (1961-1979)	28%	28%	26%
Millennials (1980-1995)	31%	33%	32%
Generation Z (1996-1998)	8%	6%	9%

Note: As we only survey those eighteen and older, Gen Z was limited to three years.

GENDER OF RESPONDENTS

Respondents were asked to identify their gender.

GENDER	OVERALL	CANADA	US
Female	52%	51%	54%
Male	46%	48%	44%
Third Gender/Unspecified/Other	2%	1%	2%

LOCATION OF RESPONDENTS

Surveys were distributed throughout the United States and

Canada. Quotas were applied to ensure a representative sample was obtained throughout both countries, with the results as follows:

UNITED STATES		CANADA	
Northeast US	28%	Western Canada	40%
South US	22%	Central Canada	35%
Midwest US	18%	Atlantic Canada	17%
West US	32%	Northern Canada	6%

Note: States/provinces have been grouped by areas.

RESPONDENT ACQUISITION

The majority of respondents (92 percent) were attracted through social media using a series of precisely worded advertisements, and participants were offered a chance to enter a prize draw for an Amazon gift card. These recruitment messages have been refined over almost a decade of trial-and-error testing.

The remaining respondents were sourced through online survey panels, predominantly to gather data for social media-related questions. We did this to minimize the potential skewing of data, which could occur if questions about social media were only posed to respondents sourced through social media channels. We also were able to see that the majority of all questions were answered by all respondents in a similar way regardless of the source. Therefore, any concern about respondents being sourced primarily through social media channels is moot.

The result was a stratified random sample with a statistical representation of the population of Canada and the USA answering the questions we needed to provide the benchmarking data, also known as the Valuegraphics Database.

DATA CLEANING AND VALIDITY CHECKS

To ensure data hygiene, a series of twelve data-cleaning methods/validity checks were implemented. We removed any surveys that seemed suspicious to avoid selection bias and data skewing. Following are just a few of the data-cleaning checks we implemented.

→ Responses completed more than 25 percent faster than the average completion time.

→ Consistent straightlining (e.g., where respondents give the same rating for each question on a matrix of questions).

→ Consistent gibberish and/or one-word answers for open-ended questions.

→ Consistent selection of only one option for multiple-selection questions.

→ Consistent selection of all options for multiple-selection questions.

→ Duplicate responses from the same respondent/IP address.

DATA ANALYSIS

Data was analyzed using a combination of Microsoft Excel, SPSS, and NVivo, and was explored both as one large data set and in relevant segments, including the Valuegraphics Archetypes. Initial analysis included a technique called *sample assessment*, which ensures the collected data is representative of the target population. Further, we employed *exploratory analysis*, a real-time assessment of incoming data to gauge perceptions of the developing data set in advance of analysis of each question.

All open-ended questions were coded, and a thematic analysis technique was used to identify key themes within the data. These themes revealed commonalities and contrasts across and within segments and cohorts. Put another way, this coding of the thematic analysis *quantified the qualitative data.*

Analysis of each question was performed using methods relevant to the format of the question. Question formats included, but were not limited to: mean ratings, spreads, distributions, and percentages. All eleven-point-scale (zero to ten) questions were both averaged and categorized as follows:

→ Ratings of nine or ten: Extremely, Strongly agree, etc.
→ Ratings of seven or eight: Somewhat agree
→ Ratings of four, five, six: Neutral, Average, etc.
→ Ratings of three or less: Unlikely, Strongly disagree, etc.

VARIABLE IDENTIFICATION AND VALUEGRAPHICS ARCHETYPE FORMULATION

Responses to each question were compared to the full Valuegraphics Database of responses to identify those that were most similar.

Similarity was measured by averaging the differences from respondents who considered their primary values to be extremely important and gave them a rating of nine or ten.* By searching for the ten key variables that resulted in the closest alignment of other responses, the ten Valuegraphics Archetypes were revealed. The primary ten Valuegraphics Archetypes' responses to all questions on all topics, for example, were similar to each other with as little disagreement as 2 percent.

The respondents within each Valuegraphics Archetype resemble each other on all things to a remarkable degree, irrespective of age and other traditional demographic categories. The discovery of these ten radically similar archetypes was our light-bulb moment. We had proven that profiling target audiences based on what people value is far more powerful than the old-fashioned demographic methods used in boardrooms everywhere today.

---

* There was one exception to this rule: in situations where variables were polar opposites (e.g., materialism vs. anti-materialism) the least important value or variable was excluded from the average calculation to avoid skewing the data in one direction.

ABOUT THE AUTHOR

DAVID ALLISON began working in advertising agencies in 1985 and helped motivate audiences for some of the world's largest brands. In 2016 he sold the ten-year-old marketing agency he had built and launched, DAVID ALLISON INC., a small global advisory firm.

He spent the next two years building Valuegraphics, the first-ever big-data tool that can profile the shared values of entire target audiences and replace outdated demographic profiling models.

Today, his company creates custom Valuegraphics Profiles from the ever-evolving database and consults with organizations who are interested in the full scope of what Valuegraphics can tell them about the audiences they want to motivate more often.

David is an author, researcher, facilitator, and advisor. He is also a frequent keynote speaker, represented by the National Speakers Bureau and the Global Speakers Agency.

Made in the USA
Columbia, SC
13 February 2021